SWANSEA
AT WAR

SWANSEA AT WAR

SALLY BOWLER

SUTTON PUBLISHING

First published in the United Kingdom in 2006 by
Sutton Publishing Limited · Phoenix Mill
Thrupp · Stroud · Gloucestershire · GL5 2BU

British Library Cataloguing in Publication Data
A catalogue record for this book is available from the British Library.

ISBN 0-7509-4464-1

Typeset in 11/13.5 Sabon.
Typesetting and origination by
Sutton Publishing Limited.
Printed and bound in England by
J.H. Haynes & Co. Ltd, Sparkford.

Contents

I would like to dedicate this book to my late parents Ken and Sadie Lewis, and to the people of Swansea, for helping us wartime children to survive against all odds.

Acknowledgements

I would like to thank all the people of my home town who took part with so much enthusiasm in the compilation of this book. I would also like to acknowledge the assistance of and photographs from Swansea Museum, the Glamorgan Archive Service, the *South Wales Evening Post* and the Gorseinon Archive and History Society. A special thanks to Dr John R. Alban, Nigel Robins, Swansea historian Royston Kneath, John and Carol Powell and Gerald Gabb.

I also thank my husband Tony and my family for their endless support throughout this project.

All pictures are from the author's own collection unless otherwise credited. Every effort has been made by the author to contact and acknowledge the copyright holder of each of the images in this book.

Introduction

Swansea, the Welsh Abertawe, is the second largest city in Wales. It stands at the mouth of the River Tawe on the edge of the Bristol Channel and looks out over Swansea Bay. The modern city stretches from The Quadrant shopping centre and the Maritime Quarters and follows the curve of the bay round to Black Pill, Oystermouth and Mumbles Pier. This was once the route of the first passenger railway in the world, known locally as 'the Mumbles Train'. The train operated from 1804 and survived many different eras of motive power until its closure in the 1960s. Today, the same Mumbles Road route takes in the Swansea University and Singleton Hospital buildings that are among the finest establishments in Wales. The road also extends to the Gower Peninsula, the first place in Britain to be designated as an Area of Outstanding Natural Beauty.

Swansea Town, which gained city status in 1969, began as a small marketplace and coal port centred on the medieval Swansea Castle. Later, Saint Mary's Parish Church joined the castle, and with the market was enclosed within the boundaries of the town walls and the narrow streets. The castle, with the church and the market, still forms the cornerstone of the modern city centre along with the immediate vicinity of Castle Square, which took the brunt of the Swansea Blitz.

Throughout the centuries of change the town has developed from being an early centre of the shipbuilding trade into a major seaport. As the advances in the eighteenth and nineteenth centuries continued, the docks expanded and the town went on to become a world-renowned trading centre. By the twentieth century Swansea had been transformed into the metallurgic capital of the world.

Before the Second World War, the late 1930s saw Swansea become a thriving industrial and commercial area. Local residents still talk of the town that was 'full of narrow, bustling streets'. It also stood at the edge of an important railway network. Having survived the Depression years, the town still reflected the outward signs of affluence and its past glories. The Castle, Saint Mary's Church and the covered market place, the largest in Wales, were still central to the town centre and Castle Bailey Street, the pre-war name of Castle Street and Castle Square.

One of the finest examples of this affluence was the prestigious Ben Evans, the town's first major department store and the largest in Wales. The five-storey building, known locally as the 'Harrods of Wales', had stood in the town centre since 1828, a symbol of Swansea's prosperity. The market had also been trading since 1828.

The town has always been proud of its many fine public buildings. Among them are Swansea Museum, the Central Library and the Glynn Vivian Art

Gallery, home of a world-famous porcelain collection. The jewel in the crown of those pre-war years was the New Guildhall, opened in 1934 and still one of Swansea's finest landmarks.

On the far side of Castle Square, the distinctive shop frontage belonged to one of the two prestigious Sidney Heath department stores. It stood opposite the Wesley Chapel in the old Goat Street that was destroyed in the blitz. The store, which specialised in school uniforms, is on the site of the house where Richard 'Beau' Nash (1673–1761) was born. A few days after the blitz, the store was one of many that lay in ruins, yet the ornate frontage still stood as if in defiance of the enemy. After the war, Sidney Heath opened larger premises, and the original building, which was renamed Beau Nash House, has retained the distinctive mock Tudor face that is seen today.

The Mumbles Train brought the early-day commuters from Mumbles into town. Shoppers also alighted from the steam trains at High Street station. Many of the residents can still recall how the town appeared in those early days. A walk from High Street to Castle Square would find streets full of individual shops. There were seats placed at the counters for the comfort of customers, who also enjoyed 'personal service' from the shop assistants. At the top of High Street there was the Elysium Cinema and the very luxurious Mackworth Hotel, with its ornate, red-and-gold-carpeted interior. Customers would shop at Lewis Lewis – the shop's double name was a fashion in those days – where you could watch the cash bells flying across the ceilings on high, thin wires. Then there was Meyler's, a draper's store, which had such an ornate and richly carved wood interior that it looked like a hotel. Other residents describe the numerous shops on the walk towards Castle Square. Snell's music shop, for instance, was part of the old High Street arcade. And there were many men's tailor's shops, including Hope Brothers and Fifty Shilling Tailors. Some shoppers took tea in the Kardomah Café and then finished their day by watching a film at the Rialto Cinema in Wind Street or the Castle Cinema in Castle Square. There were also a large number of theatres, a legacy from the Victorian era. Thus the scene is set at the very heart of the town, the district that would be devastated by the Swansea Blitz.

With the outbreak of the Second World War, the *Luftwaffe* had identified Swansea as a potential target for air raids. The metallurgic and coal industries were seen as crucial to the war effort, and Swansea Docks handled millions of tons of raw materials, foodstuffs and manufactured goods. The South Wales ports depended on the Great Western Railway for its distribution of goods in Wales as well as into England and beyond. At the same time, there were the town's steel, tinplate and lubricant industries, all with their capacity for storing aviation fluid. The town also dealt with weapons and troop reinforcements. Thus the *Luftwaffe* saw Swansea as a target of great importance. Following Hitler's failure to defeat the RAF in the Battle of Britain, and the Fall of France, the Germans began their night-time bombing campaigns. In three nights, the bombers reduced the whole of the Swansea town centre and the surrounding areas to a mass of smouldering

Swansea was a bustling town in the 1930s.

rubble. What is recorded as the worst devastation the town has suffered in the whole of its history is now known as the 'Three Nights' Blitz'.

There have been many important books written on the subject of the Swansea Blitz and the way the town came to terms with the devastation of war. The aim of my book is to tell the stories of how the Swansea people managed to get on with their everyday struggle to live normally throughout the war. It is a tribute to my own parents, and to everyone who kept the families, homes and town moving in spite of the ravages they encountered during the years that Swansea was at war.

The Marina today, part of the redevelopment of Swansea.

Gower Bay.

Swansea Castle still forms the cornerstone of the city centre.

Swansea Castle lies close to the old town centre, which took the brunt of the bombing during the Three Nights' Blitz. The neo-Tudor Sidney Heath building overlooks Castle Square, right, site of Ben Evans department store which was destroyed during the blitz.

GET IT AT

BEN EVANS'S

THE PREMIER FASHION AND FURNISHING HOUSE OF WALES AND THE WEST

TEMPLE STREET AND CASTLE BAILEY STREET FRONTAGES

38 **DEPARTMENTS**
deal comprehensively with every requirement for Personal Wear or Complete House Furnishing at prices which are the lowest anywhere for Goods of equal quality ∴.

VISITORS are invited to walk through at any time during business hours—there is no obligation whatever to purchase

BEN EVANS & Co., Ltd., SWANSEA
Telegrams "EVANS, SWANSEA"
Telephone 5015

RICHARD G. LEWIS
Managing Director

Ben Evans' advertisements were almost as elaborate as the building itself. (Courtesy Swansea Museum)

Ben Evans' store, the 'Harrods of Wales', stood as a symbol of Swansea's prosperity. (Courtesy Swansea Museum)

Statue at the Marina of Dylan Thomas, the celebrated Swansea poet.

Saint Mary's Parish Church was destroyed in the blitz and rebuilt after the war.

Swansea Docks, one of the prime targets of the wartime bombers. (Courtesy Glamorgan Archive Service)

The 'New' Guildhall, built in 1934, survived the war and remains one of Swansea's finest landmarks.

The frontage of the former Sidney Heath department store stood defiant while the shop behind and much of the surrounding area was destroyed in the blitz.

CHAPTER ONE
Preparing for War

The ack-ack units were always prepared.

By the time war was declared on 3 September 1939, preparations for Swansea's wartime defences were well under way. As the new War Minister, Oliver Stanley, took up his post at the London War Office in 1940, Swansea's wartime plans were being implemented too. Nearly two million men in the 19–28 age group were called up for active service under the terms of the Military Training Act. Unemployed men signed themselves up for active service, too. At the same time, a massive recruitment drive called for volunteers to join the departments of the volunteer wardens, ambulance drivers, rescue and first-aid parties. Others volunteered to serve in the branches of Air Raid Precautions, the ARP.

The ARP group established by the Swansea Corporation operated from their main headquarters at the Guildhall. Their duties included the sequestrating of many of the town's buildings for ARP use and coordinating the work of other emergency services. They also included the enforcement of the blackout regulations, which decreed that the windows of every house should be covered with black material in order to prevent any chink of household light being visible to enemy planes. A public information leaflet issued by the government warned 'Every occupier of rooms, house or flat is responsible for darkening his own lights.' The motto for safety was 'Keep it dark'. The leaflet also recommended the use of fabric for making blackout curtains or blinds from dark blue, black or dark green glazed Holland, Lancaster or Italian cloth. At home the blackout rules were strict, and people were fined heavily if they did not observe them. The slightest flicker of light from a window was enough to cause the ARP warden to shout 'Put that light out!'

During the pre-war years, Swansea Fire Brigade had been operated by the local police force. In 1938, almost 500 reinforcements were drafted in as the Auxiliary Fire Service, the AFS. Swansea also had three battalions of Local Defence Volunteers, later renamed the Home Guard. This was a British volunteer organisation proposed by the War Secretary, Anthony Eden, to assist in the defence of Britain against German invasion. The role of the volunteers was to defend the coastline and other strategic points such as the railways from imminent attack and invasion. The organisation was officially dissolved in December 1944.

At home, iron railings and garden gates disappeared in the drive to collect scrap metal from houses for the war effort. The tons of scrap helped towards the funds of the War Comforts Committee. Huge brick-built communal air-raid shelters appeared in many of the streets in the built-up areas. Many households were given corrugated iron Anderson shelters, which the families had to construct for themselves. At the same time, a system of air-raid warnings came into force. The colour yellow was recognised as the preliminary warning light to bring the anti-aircraft units, civil defence, firefighters and police into the preparations for emergencies. The colour red and the sounding of the air-raid siren alerted the civilian population to an imminent air raid, while a white signalled the all-clear.

However, one of the most unpopular of the wartime preparations was the gas mask, officially known as respirators, that the government had issued to over 38 million people by 1940. Although, thankfully, their use was never required during the war years, everyone had to carry them wherever they went. The government-warning posters read, 'Hitler will send no warning – so always carry your gas mask.'

The gas masks were functional black for adults and brightly coloured for children. Babies' respirators completely enclosed their bodies. Each adult gas mask was supplied in a canvas bag with a demister for the eye shields and a cardboard carrying case with a long strap. Leaflets advised the public, 'This will give you adequate protection against breathing in any of the known gases.'

Alas, food shortages due to wartime disruptions were inevitable and meant the rationing of basic food, in spite of Swansea's prosperity. When food rationing began in January 1940, every man, woman and child in Britain was issued with a ration book. Every family received a supply of ration books that recorded the limited amount of basic food to which they were entitled. Each person received food up to the value of the twenty points that were allocated to them each week. It was necessary for every household to register with a grocer, a butcher and a baker. The ration books were colour-coded according to age group: buff for adults, blue for children and green for babies. The families handed the ration books to the shopkeepers, who cut out the correct number of coupons or points.

Although the Ministry of Food changed the number of points required on a regular basis, the average weekly ration for each person was eight ounces of sugar, four ounces of butter, bacon or ham, one egg and two ounces of tea. In addition, the South Wales Divisional Food Officer, T.G. Jones, issued a public warning: 'It will be unlawful for any person to endeavour to obtain, or for any person to supply, more than the prescribed quantities.'

In 1942, the government announced the rationing of sweets and chocolate. Each person's allowance was a ration of eight ounces of sweets or chocolate, the equivalent of one bar of chocolate, every four weeks. Radio programmes, newspapers and women's magazines regularly suggested recipes for making sweets at home. The result of food rationing was the regular sight of long queues outside shops that frequently ran out of basic food supplies. Shortages were inevitable, and items like oranges and bananas became a rare luxury. Throughout the war years, the health of babies and expectant mothers remained a major priority. A baby's ration was supplemented with extra milk, meat, eggs and fresh oranges. The introduction of the Welfare Foods Scheme also meant that mothers and their babies had an extra supply of blackcurrant juice, cod liver oil and, later on, bottles of orange juice.

As the war progressed and the shortages continued, the Women's Land Army promoted the 'Dig for Victory' campaign. People were urged to use their gardens and allotments to grow vegetables that would supplement the food shortages. Posters read, 'Your bread costs ships.' Signs appeared all over town urging people to eat home-grown potatoes. Many people recall eating the local delicacy of laver bread, whose basic ingredient is the edible seaweed that grows in abundance along the miles of rocky Gower coastline.

As rationing began, shops soon ran out of supplies. Long queues became a common sight.

Clothes rationing meant that coupons were also needed to buy new garments. Although mothers received extra coupons for nappies and baby clothes, each person received an average allowance of about forty-eight coupons a year. In the shops, the coupon value was pinned to each garment. For example, a sweater was five coupons, a skirt, four coupons, and a pair of trousers, six coupons. Many people became adept at unpicking and remodelling clothes. They also spent hours unravelling old knitwear to make into new items. It began a craze of 'make do and mend' that would last well into the next decade. Groups of people at work also knitted garments for the serving military forces. Many of them organised concerts, whist drives and football matches to help the War Comforts Fund. A consignment of parcels was sent regularly to the Swansea men of the BEF (British Expeditionary Force). They included comforts such as socks, scarves, razor blades, toothpaste, soap, chewing gum and newspapers.

Magazines and newspapers suggested recipes and household saving tips.

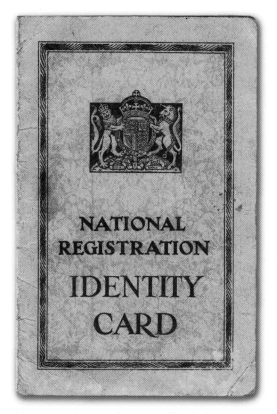

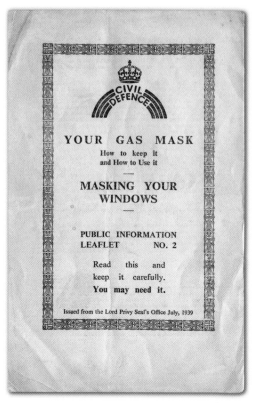

Identity cards were shown to officials for inspection.

The gas mask was an unpopular apparatus yet it was considered vital in saving lives.

MASKING YOUR WINDOWS

In war, one of our great protections against the dangers of air attack after nightfall would be the " black-out." On the outbreak of hostilities all external lights and street lighting would be totally extinguished so as to give hostile aircraft no indication as to their whereabouts. But this will not be fully effective unless *you* do your part, and see to it that no lighting in the house where you live is visible from the outside. The motto for safety will be " Keep it dark ! "

Every occupier of rooms, house or flat would be responsible for darkening his own lights. Lights in the halls or on the staircases of blocks of flats or dwellings would be the responsibility of the landlord or owner.

Of course, the most convenient way of shutting in the light is to use close fitting blinds. These can be of any thick, dark coloured material such as dark blue or black or dark green glazed Holland, Lancaster or Italian Cloth.

If you cannot manage this, you could obscure your windows by fixing up sheets of black paper or thick dark brown paper mounted on battens.

Blackout rules were strict during the Second World War and heavy fines were imposed on people who broke them.

HM Revenue & Customs

Here is your new tax code for 2009-10

It will be used by your employer or pension provider from 6 April 2009

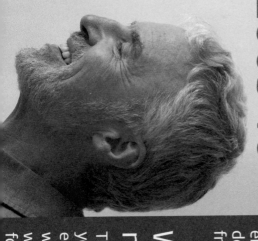

Why do I need a new tax code?

Your new tax code ensures your employer or pension provider deducts the right amount of tax from your income.

What do I need to do?

This Coding Notice is simply for you to keep. We will tell your employer or pension provider what your new tax code is. And we will notify any agent acting for you as well.

Please go to
www.hmrc.gov.uk/incometax

more information?

Please read all the notes on
your Coding Notice. You can
find out more about income
tax, allowances, taxable
benefits and tax codes on
our website.

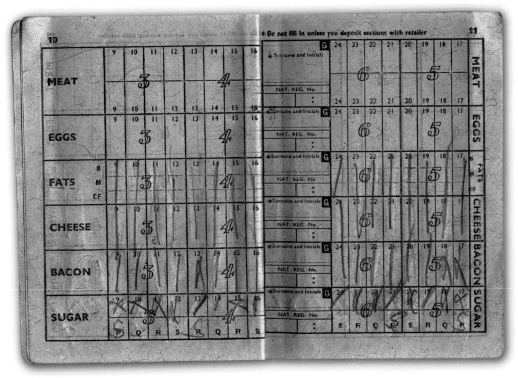

Shopkeepers cut out the coupons from the ration books. The rations or 'points' were recognised by the numbered pages.

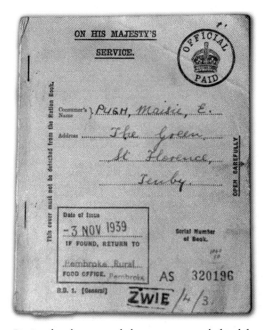

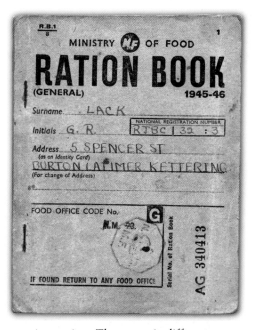

Ration books ensured there was enough food for everyone in wartime. They came in different colours: buff for adults, blue for children and green for babies.

Bananas became a rare sight in the war.

There was a different system of rationing for fats and cooking oils.

CHAPTER TWO

Keep on Moving

Car drivers faced petrol shortages as well as hazardous road restrictions.

With the wartime rationing of petrol and oil, motorists were restricted to travelling 'only if they considered their journeys were necessary'. The drivers of all road vehicles had to fit masks over their headlights, which limited the illumination to little more than the sidelights. At the same time, the removal of all street direction signs aimed to make it difficult for potential land invasion enemies to establish where they were. Every road-junction sign and every nameplate for town or village was removed. Shop signs and those which included a place name were painted over. Swansea signs were reduced to boards with white lettering on a black background. These indicated 'S' for air-raid shelter, 'FAP' for first-aid post and 'EWS' for emergency water supply.

Naturally, the blackout restrictions, reduced street lighting and dimmed vehicle lights contributed to the cause of many road accidents. Yet, in spite of the rationing and the strict traffic regulations, vehicles played a major part in the war effort. The Mumbles Train was more popular than ever among its wartime passengers. The electrically powered trains were unaffected by petrol rationing and wartime restrictions. Great steps were taken to ensure the safety of both the passengers and trains as well as the railway lines. The trains were stored at several locations along the route, from the terminus at Rutland Street in Swansea to Mumbles Pier, so as to minimise the potential damage to the service during the air raids. A line was opened into the Clyne Valley so that the train could be hidden in the woodland in the event of a bombardment.

The normal restrictions to the number of passengers allowed on the train were also relaxed. This meant that there were often so many people waiting at the Rutland Street terminus that the ticket collectors found it impossible to collect the fares on the crowded trains. On many occasions they attempted to collect the fares from the people standing in the queues. They also allowed passengers with season tickets to board the train first. In general, the passengers were good-humoured and only too grateful for any form of transport, whatever the inconvenience. Many of them still have a high regard for those who kept the Mumbles Train moving during those darkest days.

John Wright from Mumbles recalled how the amount of fuel allocated for buses was much less than before the war. The bus companies were expected to provide public-transport vehicles on demand for the military purposes. They were also required to run additional services taking workers to the factories. Internal lighting in buses was also reduced. Bus companies issued their conductors with torches to illuminate their ticket machines. During an air raid, the buses, as with all road vehicles, were required to stop and extinguish all lights. If bombing activities were close then drivers urged passengers to dismount and disperse behind hedges or other natural cover and wait until they heard the all-clear.

During the early years of the war, orders went out that vehicles were to be commandeered from private owners and businesses for use as ambulances and fire engines and for other civilian purposes.

The Mumbles Train continued to operate throughout the war years. It was one of the most popular forms of public transport. (Courtesy Swansea Museum)

John Pressdee, owner of the local undertakers and taxi firm, lives in Bishopston and remembers the situation well. When the Second World War began, he was a 9-year-old school pupil. On one occasion he was in his grandfather's garage and undertakers business in Stanley Street, Mumbles. He can remember the day, just at the start of the war, when the Mumbles Auxiliary Fire Service officers arrived at the garage to commandeer the garage vehicles for AFS use. John described it as being exciting for a child, but it must have been stressful for the owners, who regarded their vehicles not only as their pride and joy, but as an essential component of their business. He recalls:

Two of the cars were funeral cars that belonged to my grandfather Alfred Pressdee. The only payment he was offered was £25 each, which was eventually received after the war. This seemed small in comparison with their current market value of £500 each, although, even then, the cars were never

John Pressdee, the small boy standing to the right of the picture, was 9 years old when the Auxiliary Fire Service (AFS) arrived. (Courtesy John Pressdee)

returned, as one was destroyed by enemy action at Pembroke Dock. As for the other car, we never saw it again. Besides the cars, half my grandfather's garage was also requisitioned for use as a fire station. It was also fitted out as living accommodation, and used as billets for the fire officers. An air-raid siren was fitted just outside my bedroom window. I remember how my peers kept trying to make me go into the air-raid shelter. Even as a child, I kept thinking it was crazy and refused to go into it because I had heard that the shelters were built on top of two petrol tanks. I believed that one bomb could have blown us all sky high.

John's father Bill Pressdee was in the army, so it was his mother Doris who helped to keep the old family business going throughout the war. She even drove the hearse, using her Austin Twelve car as the family business vehicle and as a taxi, and covering many miles.

As a small boy, John found the blitz an awesome sight as he stood looking across the bay from Mumbles to where he could see the many fires burning over Swansea:

I would aim potshots with my toy air rifle at the planes, although I knew I would have a fat chance of hitting them. There were the ack-ack guns at Mumbles Head that tried their best to defend the Mumbles shoreline. But I remember wondering if they did more damage to Mumbles than they did to the enemy, although the real enemy action meant that many local houses had cracks in their walls. I remember the ceilings coming down in my own house in Stanley Street and just missing my sister's cot.

John also remembers the Surrey Regiment in Underhill Park, and recalls the time when the Americans arrived in Swansea:

I saw a large number of American troops. Many of them were stationed, and lived under canvas, in Caswell Bay. We found the Americans were very generous and would give us kids Hershey Bars and chewing gum. They also gave us tins of meat, which they threw from their lorries to us kids standing at the side of the road. This is also the way I had my first sight of a grapefruit.

Austin breakdown truck, used as a fire engine. (Courtesy John Pressdee)

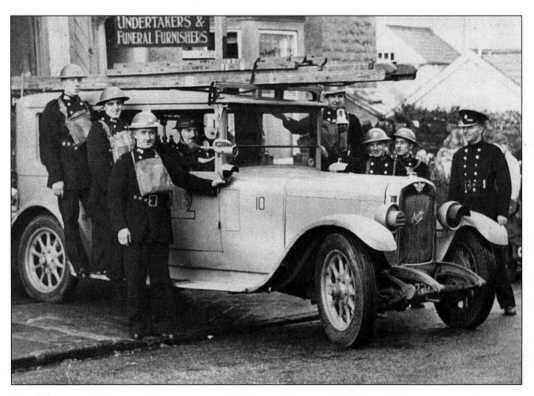

Fire-fighters used stirrup pumps to put out the flames. (Courtesy John Pressdee)

Private vehicles were often commandered for use as ambulances or fire engines.

John Pressdee's mother, Doris, kept the family firm going by driving her Austin Twelve as a business vehicle and taxi. (Courtesy John Pressdee)

Bus companies were expected to operate additional services on a limited fuel allocation. (Courtesy Swansea City Council)

CHAPTER THREE

The Three Nights' Blitz

After the Three Nights' Blitz, fire fighters found the resulting fires almost impossible to control. (Courtesy Swansea Museum)

The Three Nights' Blitz describes the three nights of sustained bombing of Swansea by the German *Luftwaffe* during the Second World War. The blitz caused widespread death and injuries, and massive destruction. More than 11,000 homes and businesses were demolished, and the whole town centre was destroyed. The blitz took place on the nights of 19–21 February 1941.

The first air raids on Swansea had occurred in 1940, shortly after the Fall of France. Although the bombers attacked the town on more than forty occasions, the Three Nights' Blitz was the most severe of the war and the town's worst ordeal in its entire history. The first enemy aircraft arrived overhead at midnight. Their task was to illuminate the targets by means of parachute flares and incendiary bombs. The dropped parachutes hung over the town and lit up the area for miles around. The bomber planes followed and, guided by the light of the flares, found it easy to locate their targets. For the three nights of the Swansea blitz, the bombers dropped a mixture of high explosives and incendiaries on the town centre and the surrounding areas. In no time the town was ablaze and fires raged out of control. Firefighters fought heroically against the inferno, with the added hazards of unexploded bombs and falling buildings making their job even more difficult. People reported seeing the glow from the burning town as far away as the west Wales and Devonshire coastlines.

In all the bombing raids lasted for nearly fourteen hours, at the end of which more than forty acres of the town and the surrounding area had been reduced to rubble. Over 200 people alone died in the bombing of Wesley Chapel in the old Goat Street. The Ben Evans store was reduced to an empty shell. Castle Square, Saint Mary's Church and the surrounding buildings in Caer Street and Temple Street were completely destroyed. The glass-covered market was also damaged by incendiary bombs that destroyed the roof and interior walls of the building, even though the outer walls remained intact.

Swansea Castle remained untouched by the raids, as did Salubrious Passage, a medieval walk barely minutes away. The bombers left the docks and the surrounding industries undamaged, and many people questioned why they had struck at the town centre instead. One of the theories was that the bombers were diverted from their targets by the sudden sight of the steep rise of Kilvey Hill, which looms over 600ft above the east side of the town. However, the writings of Dr John R. Alban suggest another, more likely, theory as the reason why Swansea was targeted for enemy attacks: the town's metallurgic and coal industries were crucial to the war effort and, most importantly, Swansea was a storage point for aviation fluid. Perhaps the bombers simply missed their targets.

In comparison, the British fighters on the ground also lacked the advanced technology they needed to respond to the constant attacks by the German bombers. At the time, the Luftwaffe possessed the most powerful bomber fleet in the world. This meant that the crucial night-time means of defence fell to the anti-aircraft units of the Royal Artillery. Their main weapon of defence was the anti-aircraft or ack-ack gun. The gun was supported by searchlights beamed upwards, which

Ben Evans was left as an empty shell. (Courtesy Swansea Museum)

became a familiar sight across the Swansea skies. In this way, the men were able to identify the approach of the German bomber planes at night.

One part of Castle Street commemorates the 'Castle Street Bomb', the scene of one of the great tragedies of the blitz. On the third night of the bombing raids, six young bomb-disposal men died while they were dealing with one of the many unexploded bombs that fell all over the town. Another major tragedy occurred at Teilo Crescent, Mayhill, when a whole barrage of bombs was dropped onto a row of houses that were already in flames from an earlier air raid. Firefighters and ARP wardens as well as many of the street's residents were killed.

After the bombing raids, the private houses in the residential area of Walters Road were turned into shops so that the shopkeepers could continue their businesses. It was also essential to replace the bombed-out market, a major food

The market's glass roof and interior was destroyed. (Courtesy South Wales Evening Post)

supply, as soon as possible. Within a week of the blitz, the borough's estates department had established a temporary market place on the upper floors of the site of the old United Welsh bus station in Singleton Street. Many of the makeshift stalls were made out of packing cases in which aircraft parts had been imported.

After the Food Office in Northampton Lane, the town's main provision centre, was bombed, all the paperwork, books and public records were lost. The office was soon replaced. The Women's Voluntary Service workers rallied to get the kitchens in the Old Guildhall going. The staff from the bombed-out Food Office were among the first to offer their help. One of the main concerns was to keep up the work of stoking the boilers in the Guildhall and to ensure there was a continuous supply of hot water.

The volunteers also prepared food in the kitchens, which was loaded onto mobile canteens. The mobile canteens were vans with a cab holding a stove and tea urns. The drivers distributed hot meals and drinks to help boost the morale of the people in the bombed-out areas. For the same reason, cafes opened in Nelson Street and Alexander Road where people whose houses had been bombed could buy cheap, hot meals. Dinners were served regularly and people with little money were given free meals. It meant that people could keep on working and maintain their high levels of production.

Part of Swansea Castle which faced the town centre and survived the wartime air raids.

Part of the medieval Salubrious Passage as it is today. Miraculously, the castle, cinema and nearby passageway were untouched by the bombs.

The old Evening Post *building in Castle Bailey Street faces a scene of devastation.* (Courtesy *South Wales Evening Post*)

Castle Street and the once prosperous town centre after the Three Nights' Blitz. (Courtesy R. Wood)

A town destroyed. (Courtesy R. Wood)

Unexploded bomb warning signs appeared in nearly every street. The sign was one of many that warned the public of the dangers after the blitz.

CHAPTER FOUR

Lieutenant William George Bladen

Lt George Bladen led the fire picquet throughout the nights of the blitz.
(Courtesy John and Carol Powell)

Lieutenant William George Bladen, Commanding Officer of 5 Platoon, lived at Rhondda Street, Mount Pleasant. He had served in the First World War. During the Second World War, he was a Home Guard leader of the fire piquet at Swansea's Central Hall. The following are edited excerpts from his first-hand account of the members of the piquet, transcribed from a handwritten copy he left to his granddaughter, Mrs Carol Powell. It records the nights of 21–22 February 1941, describing the terrifying events that occurred and the men who stayed and faced the hour-by-hour devastation of the Three Nights' Blitz. Lieutenant Bladen writes:

The piquet was mounted at 19.00 hours and in accordance with battalion orders. The Picquet was divided into three sections, each one under the command of an NCO. There were also runners detailed for the police and AFS, the Auxiliary Fire Service, and the duties of the FP [fire picquet] read out. The air-raid alert sounded at 19.50 hours and a guard of two men within minutes was posted on the main entrance. Within minutes, I received a message that flares were being dropped by the enemy aircraft, and immediately went out into the street to see what was happening . . . a shower of incendiaries came down. Incendiary bomb drops on the roof at the rear of the HQ company office. Incendiary lodges in roof, resulting fire being tackled by Dan Hansen, RSM Mugford and others. The whole of the Piquet is now in action . . . fire in window of wine shop in Gower Street, fire in window of gent's outfitters in College Street, incendiaries galore outside the Central Hall, all being dealt with by the Fire Picquet, notwithstanding the fact that HEs [high explosives] were being dropped in the immediate vicinity. One civilian and two soldiers being killed whilst sheltering in Orchard Street – three doors away from the Central Hall . . .

Lieutenant Bladen's account continues:

I now receive a message that Capel Gomer (next to Central Hall) is on fire inside. I immediately muster four or five men with a stirrup pump and buckets of water and inside we went. I at once saw the position was hopeless – there before us was the organ well on fire and the roof ablaze. Realising we could do no good with the SP [stirrup pump] and that it would be dangerous to leave men there trying to fight the fire, I ordered them back to the Hall. We had just returned to the entrance Hall when an HE dropped, well I should say, somewhere at the rear of the Capel Gomer, as the debris simply pounded down on the Central Hall . . .

Lieutenant Bladen describes how, during this time, a message was sent by Sgt R.G. Wray to the Central Police Station asking for help and for firefighting appliances. The message that came back was that nothing could be done as there was no water supply. Bladen also records that the only way to deal with an incendiary bomb discovered 'burning at the top of the Central Hall was for one man to put his head and shoulders through the window. Then take with him the nozzle of the stirrup pump, and to form a chain of buckets of water up the steps.' His handwritten notes continue:

During this period most of the premises in Orchard Street was on fire. Waterloo Street was a mass of fire from side to side . . . Gower Street was well ablaze, also College Street. As far as one could see, the whole district was ablaze. I do not think I am exaggerating when I say that the whole of the town centre was all ablaze by 21.00 hours . . . I then decided that the piquet should muster at the bottom of High Street if possible and go through College Street before vacating the Hall. I endeavoured to ring up Major Kydd to inform him of my actions but could not get through as the telephone wires were down . . . Most of the Hall now well alight, part of the same having been previously blown off. With Sgt Wray, [volunteer] A.J. Jones and a few others we then made our way through College Street to High Street. It was certainly a case of keeping going or be burnt . . . I now wanted to get to the Central Police Station so [as] to have temporary headquarters and to communicate with Major Kydd. To do so we had to go down Welcome Lane, up the Strand . . . to arrive at the PS [police station] . . .

There was now a lull in the bombing and, realising the men and women as well as myself would like to go home for a while to see if their wives and families were all right, we did so. Now, outside, there was part of the BBC roof on fire – Trinity Church roaring furnace – a house opposite on fire – De la Beche school a mass of fire . . . With Sgt Wray, we now proceeded up Mount Pleasant Hill . . . to see the grammar school on fire. Getting near our homes . . . everything seemed so quiet . . . as if miles away from the town, yet it was only ten minutes away. We found a bomb had completely demolished a house in Terrace Road . . . a house in Norfolk Street was demolished . . . Down below in Heathfield several bombs had fallen. To our joy we arrived in Rhondda Street to find all safe after a terrifying night. We now decided to go into the streets and give what help we could – assisted the AFS fighting a fire in Orchard Street . . . Proceeded to Central Hall only to find a roaring furnace. We now go down High Street, there some of the buildings down across road, others on fire . . . Back in Orchard Street, we come across a firefighter, very tired playing a hose on a building. We had just taken over the hose from him when we hear a bomb coming down . . . we duck and there is a terrific explosion. The bombers . . . had dropped this one (which was the last one that morning) on a building in High Street – Stones Wireless Shop. Knowing we had done all that was possible, the party was dismissed at approx. 5.30 a.m.

On 21 February 1941, the third night of the Swansea Blitz, Carol Powell's father Harold Symmons, a 20-year-old, was on leave and trying to get to his family home

George Bladen's handwritten notes left to his granddaughter, Carol Powell. (Courtesy John and Carol Powell)

in Rhondda Street, Mount Pleasant. He writes, 'I was worried about my wife and my in-laws. We had recently got married, on January 4th, and I was by now in Cardington, Bedfordshire awaiting embarkation, when I heard on the BBC radio of the attack on Swansea.'

After managing to get a pass, Harold caught the train from London. Reaching Pyle, he could see from the train window that the whole of Swansea appeared to be on fire.

When the train came to Neath, the Swansea passengers were told to get out because the train was not going any further. Frantic with worry, he managed to hitch a lift with some army personnel who drove him into the bomb-stricken town, where he saw that 'the whole area seemed to be on fire'.

He also found himself faced with smoke and debris from falling buildings. There were roadblocks, with signs warning the public of unexploded bombs every step of the way. Reaching the bottom of Mount Pleasant Hill, he saw even more devastation: 'Houses in Norfolk Street had been destroyed,' he writes. 'When I reached my house in Rhondda Street, another shock awaited me when a man in uniform I recognised as George Bladen opened the front door. Imagine my relief when I found out that my new wife and family were safe.'

Another account came from Ray Powell, Carol's father-in-law. Throughout the 1930s, Ray was a butcher in Eastman's in the old Goat Street arcade. On the first two nights of the blitz, Powell and the shop staff were stranded in the shop after the air-raid warning siren had sounded. It meant that they slept in the cellar of the

I n the years when our Country

was in mortal danger

William George Bladen

who served 18 May 1940 – 31 December 1944.

gave generously of his time and

powers to make himself ready

for her defence by force of arms

and with his life if need be.

George R.I.

THE HOME GUARD

shop. On the third night, for some reason we do not know, he and his staff decided to walk to his home in West Cross, which is roughly a 5-mile journey from the town centre and almost the whole length of Mumbles Road. That night the town centre was blitzed, and the next day, as his account concluded, 'the shop did no longer exist'.

My late Father-in-law's reminiscences.

My father-in-law, Ray Powell was a butcher in Eastmer's in Goat's St. Arcade, in the 30s.

On the first two nights of the blitz, they were stranded in the shop after the siren had sounded, and slept in the cellar of the shop. On the third night, for some reason we do not know, he and his staff decided to walk to his home in the West Cross Area, to spend the night.

That night Swansea Centre was extensively bombed and the next day the shop did not exist!!

Soon he was called up and served in the RAF. On his return, this advertisement appeared in the Evening Post.

Ray Powell's reminiscences of the Three Nights' Blitz. (Courtesy John and Carol Powell)

The fire picquet personnel list showing those present on the night of the blitz. (Courtesy John and Carol Powell)

IMPORTANT
WAR DATES

1939

SEP 1. Germany invaded Poland

SEP 3. Great Britain and France declared war on Germany; the B.E.F. began to leave for France

DEC 13. Battle of the River Plate

1940

APR 9. Germany invaded Denmark and Norway

MAY 10. Germany invaded the Low Countries

JUNE 3. Evacuation from Dunkirk completed

JUNE 8. British troops evacuated from Norway

JUNE 11. Italy declared war on Great Britain

JUNE 22. France capitulated

JUNE 29. Germans occupied the Channel Isles

AUG 8–OCT 31. German air offensive against Great Britain (Battle of Britain)

OCT 28. Italy invaded Greece

NOV 11–12. Successful attack on the Italian Fleet in Taranto Harbour.

DEC 9–11. Italian invasion of Egypt defeated at the battle of Sidi Barrani

1941

MAR 11. Lease-Lend Bill passed in U.S.A.

MAR 28. Battle of Cape Matapan

APR 6. Germany invaded Greece

APR 12–DEC 9. The Siege of Tobruk

MAY 20. Formal surrender of remnants of Italian Army in Abyssinia

MAY 20–31. Battle of Crete

MAY 27. German battleship *Bismarck* sunk

JUNE 22. Germany invaded Russia

AUG 12. Terms of the Atlantic Charter agreed

NOV 18. British offensive launched in the Western Desert

DEC 7. Japanese attacked Pearl Harbour

DEC 8. Great Britain and United States of America declared war on Japan

1942

FEB 15. Fall of Singapore

APR 16. George Cross awarded to Malta

OCT 23–NOV 4. German-Italian army defeated at El Alamein

NOV 8. British and American forces landed in North Africa

1943

JAN 31. The remnants of the 6th German Army surrendered at Stalingrad

MAY Final victory over the U-Boats in the Atlantic

MAY 13. Axis forces in Tunisia surrendered

JULY 10. Allies invaded Sicily

SEP 3. Allies invaded Italy

SEP 8. Italy capitulated

DEC 26. *Scharnhorst* sunk off North Cape

1944

JAN 22. Allied troops landed at Anzio

JUNE 4. Rome captured

JUNE 6. Allies landed in Normandy

JUNE 13. Flying-bomb (V.1) attack on Britain started

JUNE Defeat of Japanese invasion of India

AUG 25. Paris liberated

SEP 3. Brussels liberated

SEP 8. The first rocket-bomb (V.2) fell on England.

SEP 17–26. The Battle of Arnhem

OCT 20. The Americans re-landed in the Philippines

1945

JAN 17. Warsaw liberated

MAR 20. British recaptured Mandalay

MAR 23. British crossed the Rhine

APR 25. Opening of Conference of United Nations at San Francisco

MAY 2. German forces in Italy surrendered

MAY 3. Rangoon recaptured

MAY 5. All the German forces in Holland, N.W. Germany and Denmark surrendered unconditionally

MAY 9. Unconditional surrender of Germany to the Allies ratified in Berlin

JUNE 10. Australian troops landed in Borneo

AUG 6. First atomic bomb dropped on Hiroshima

AUG 8. Russia declared war on Japan

AUG 9. Second atomic bomb dropped on Nagasaki

AUG 14. The Emperor of Japan broadcast the unconditional surrender of his country

SEP 5. British forces re-entered Singapore

MY FAMILY'S WAR RECORD

A record of the events of the Second World War. (Courtesy Gorseinon Archive and History Society)

CHAPTER FIVE

Weaver's Flour Mill at War

Weaver's Flour Mill, a Swansea institution. (Courtesy The Glamorgan Archives Service)

As everyone in Swansea knows, Weaver's and Company Flour Mill was an institution. The mill was a large grain store and processing plant, built in 1897 by the French engineer François Hennibique, and stood near the North Dock on a site now occupied by Sainsbury's supermarket. The company made flour from imported wheat and then distributed its processed products to the many bakers in the town and beyond. Weaver's siren announced the works' start, lunch-break and finishing times for decades before the war. Then the role of the mill's siren became the sound of the wartime air-raid warnings. However, such was the importance of Weaver's Flour Mill in the local food chain that the German *Luftwaffe* regarded it as a major target during the Second World War.

Mr Dee S., as he wishes to be known, was 16 years old when he started work at Weaver's in 1940. Although he went into the army later, he did not know then that he would remain working in the milling industry for the next forty-two years. He recalls the importance of the part that the flour mill and the people who worked in the industry played during the war:

Not many people realised that of all the rationing and shortages of food that occurred during the war, bread [which was only rationed for a short while after the war] was the only foodstuff that was in a continuous supply. It was indeed one of the biggest morale boosters during the wartime years. So long as people could buy bread, they were able to endure the greatest hardships. When there was no butter, the bread was spread with jam or dripping. Many people made meals from gravy poured onto a slice of bread for basic hunger relief.

The road connecting Quay Parade to the mill yard was called the Slip Road. It ran the full length of the mill building and was the cornerstone to many of the area's landmarks, such as the Cuba, a public house known to all seafarers worldwide. Adjoining the Cuba was a row of six to eight cottages, then an unused assay office that stood opposite the mill entrance. Then, on the opposite side of the Cuba was the entrance to a warehouse basement, which ran the full length of the flour warehouse above it, and from which lorry drivers drove to the basement to be loaded. There was an air-raid shelter in the basement, which Weaver's employees rarely occupied. This is because, when an air raid was in progress, everyone was engaged in the fire-watching/ firefighting activities. The people who lived in the cottages, the mill's day workers, used the shelter regularly.

As cleaners, our duties were putting the lights out in certain parts of the building. It also meant taking down the blackouts from the windows and watching the activities that went on in the assay office, and the friendly arguments that went on outside the Cuba.

In the initial stages of the Swansea air raids it was the practice that, when the air-raid warning siren sounded, the mill would shut down and the personnel would head for the shelter. However, because of the high risk of fire when incendiary bombs were dropped, everyone acted as fire-watchers. This is also because Swansea was on the flight path of the enemy aircraft that were on bombing raids from the airfields in France to the Midlands and beyond.

However, this practice proved costly to the mill in lost production. Thus the decision was made for two of the shift personnel to be posted onto the flat roof as a protection for the 'spotters' against anti-aircraft shrapnel. In theory the idea was good, but the practice caused problems. Firstly, if the bomb dropped nearby, it was too late to prevent the damage. It meant that the 'spotters' became blasé or brave about it. Secondly, [because of] the nature of the method of production, crash-stopping the mill in full flow caused considerable product loss and a great deal of exertion for the mill staff to resume full production. Likewise, the 'spotters' were subjected to a few choice words if they did stop the mill and there was no further enemy activity. Because of the system of milling in a large mill, the six floors of Weaver's were crammed with machinery for various uses in the process. These machines created a lot of noise and heat and, under peacetime working conditions, the windows opened for cooling fresh air. Under wartime conditions, all the windows at night were blacked out, so the working environment was often unpleasant. There was also the worry that if an alarm sounded, sometimes it was hard to hear because of the noise. It meant that every unusual noise made the imagination run riot. The combination of flour and grain dust is extremely explosive. Given the right conditions, fire or sparks could have caused explosions, which did not help the nerves.

One of the night-time air raids on Swansea subjected the town to extensive high-explosive and incendiary attacks. The mill was stopped after a number of incendiaries dropped on the premises had been dealt with by the mill staff. One part of the floor at the top part of the building was found to have borne the scars of the raid when it was demolished after the war.

After these incidents were over, another fire was discovered in the section that held 3,000 tons of wheat. The only access to the building was by a straight iron ladder that ran vertically to the roof gully, which had an opening along its length. The call went up to get the hosepipes out, and with more enthusiasm than experience we young lads responded by climbing along the length of the hydrant in the roof opening. From here, we ran the hosepipe lengths out, struggling up the ladder with the only light [which] came from the effects of the ack-ack gun flashes, searchlight glare and explosions. It was only then that we realised the hosepipes had not been run out properly and the section couplings had to be changed to put the fires out.

After one of the air raids, I arrived for work at the mill the following morn-ing to find that many of the slates had been blown off the roof and nearly all the windows had been damaged. However, like other mill workers, I set to work clearing up, even though I had spent the night before fire-watching at my own home in Landore. As you can imagine, the debris, a mixture of flour with glass and water, made a horrific mess. By the next day, tarpaulin was draped over the roof frame as a temporary cover. Finally, the wheels started turning again.

There was a bridge, which crossed over the main road from the mill to St Thomas. It carried a system of conveyors moving products from one side of the road to the other. Mainly, it carried wheat that was required for the mill from the grain silo that stood on the present-day Sainsbury's site to the flour warehouse. The conveyors continued through the warehouse and entered another identical bridge spanning the old Beaufort Dock to the wheat store that supplied the mill properly. Incendiary bombs dropped on the area and destroyed the bridge.

The scars made by the steel bridge crashing down and imbedding in the warehouse wall were visible until the building was demolished. Dee was working at the mill during the week of the Three Nights' Blitz. The mill site buildings, being high and sprawling, stood out from everything around them. Yet, despite from the incendiary damage that was dealt with by the mill staff, the mill continued to run in spite of the bombing raids. The employees were always very conscientious. Regardless of their own wartime problems, there were always those who volunteered for further duties. Once, there was a request from the Swansea General Hospital for two or three mill workers to act as fire-watchers there during the weekends. This was to allow the Auxiliary Fire Service officers a break from their duties. Dee was one of the people to volunteer regularly whenever mill working times allowed. The men were also required to help move heavy or large objects. Whenever there was an air-raid warning, another of the regular jobs was helping to move the children from the ward to their hospital's basement air-raid shelter.

WEAVER'S HOME GUARD

The Weaver's Home Guard began their training by using broomsticks. The men were issued with uniforms only as the items became available. That meant when it came to the exercises that some of them wore tunics, others the boots or the uniform trousers. The men in this 'Dad's Army'-type parade were quite a sight in the early days. There were about forty men in the Company, all with different working backgrounds. This was fine during working time. When it came to the army ranking, it was a different matter. There was a large age gap between the lads not yet 19-plus, the official age for military service, and men who were too old for the services even though quite a few of them had served in the First World War. The experienced men claimed that because of their military service they were the ones who should be chosen for promotion up the ranks. At times, the men working amicably together all day would suddenly want to be in charge on the Home Guard parade.

One Sunday morning, the men were practising loading and unloading their rifles when someone decided they should try live ammunition to give them experience. The sergeant barked out the orders to make them feel like real soldiers. Dee explains: 'As you could guess, one overzealous person thought he had unloaded the gun and he pulled the trigger. As the shot imbedded itself in the roof, the instructor and the men threw themselves to the floor. Thankfully, no one was hurt.'

He continues:

The Central Hall in the middle of town was the headquarters for the area Home Guard. During the night, two people were detailed from one of the Home Guard units in the area to operate the telephone messages. One night, one of our sergeants and I became the detail. We had both just dozed off when we were awakened by the ringing of the telephone. Suddenly, there were officers of all ranks around us and the place became a frantic buzz of activity. We discovered that it was the night when it was believed generally that Operation Sea Lion [the invasion of Britain] was about to take place.

On the night of the air raid, a parachute mine fell in the Strand, behind High Street Woolworth store, which is now Argos. The Home Guard on duty there were standing outside the guardroom. This was situated at one end of the canteen/mess room, which stood in Weaver's Mill yard, near to where the coal was dumped. When they looked between the gunfire flashes, they saw something drifting towards them on a parachute. Immediately, they thought that someone had baled out of the enemy plane and was about to land at their feet. Fortunately for them the object remained airborne until it landed in the Strand. For at the same time, the guards saw their moment of glory and charged over the coal heaps to make their 'capture'. The massive explosion came without warning and almost blew them over as they dived for cover. When the men had recovered from the shock, they found themselves covered with coal dust and made their way back to the mill yard. There they found the mill production had stopped and the workers who had assembled in the yard gave the guards stick for weeks afterwards.

Beyond the mill's perimeter wall to the north of the docks, there was a large area of derelict wasteland. Someone decided that this would be just the place for a night-time Home Guard exercise. The idea was that the two sides, a team of about twenty men from the company, should split into two groups and 'attack' each other. The aim was to see if they could pass each other without detection. The exercise was going well until one of the group yelled out that he had put his hand into some horse manure. The lance corporal in charge warned him to 'keep quiet'. However, the man was adamant and replied, 'If I am going to risk becoming a prisoner of war, I am not crawling about in *that* mess.' With that, he stood up and stalked off to wash his hands.

Just before the Quay Parade, on the dockside, there was an Electricity Board sub/switching station manned by one of the Board's employees. As this was the road we patrolled on our Home Guard patrols, we came to know each other. We usually stopped for a chat and a welcome cup of tea. It was good until, one cold wet night, our two-man patrol and the electrician fell asleep. We were all reprimanded by the Home Guard Commander as he was about to organise a search party, believing we had fallen into the dock.

Dee also recalls:

On Christmas Day 1941, the Guard Commander and I, along with five other soldiers, were on a twelve-hour shift of duty. At lunchtime, the Home Guard Command Officer [Mr C. Natrass], also the mill manager, came down to the mill and invited the seven of us to his office for Christmas lunch. It was quite a large feast considering it was wartime, and even included turkey and a glass of beer. The manager's office was on the ground floor of a small cottage that stood on the Quay Parade. During the meal, we discovered that two elderly sisters occupied the upstairs room. Unbeknown to anyone, Mr Natrass had arranged for the sisters to prepare the meal for us. We all thought it was a very kind gesture and typical of the good relationships that existed between the management and the workers at Weaver's Flour Mill.

CHAPTER SIX

Norma Ferguson

Norma as a nurse aged 17. (Courtesy Norma Ferguson)

Norma Ferguson, 2006.

At the beginning of the Second World War, Norma Ferguson was 17 years old and living with her parents in St Thomas. She had just started work as a nurse in the Cimla Hospital near Neath. Every day, through the continuous threat of bombing raids, Norma caught the bus from Swansea to Neath to carry out her duties. At that time she helped with the treatment of the many patients who during that era spent long and tedious months recovering in the tuberculosis ward. She recalled how on the first night of the Swansea Blitz she was at home on a few days' leave from her hospital work. That day, she and her friends had decided to take the bus into the town centre. They had looked forward to shopping in their favourite stores, such as Ben Evans and David Evans, as well as the Woolworth store that stood in High Street where Argos is today.

The group of friends boarded the bus in St Thomas for the short ride along Fabian Way and Wind Street, a bustling, narrow route compared with the magnitude of the modern road system today. As they headed for the town centre, they were chatting about the latest fashion for the Winston Churchill-inspired all-in-one garment known as the 'siren suit', and hooded coats. There were bargains, too, in the numerous 'gowns and mantles' departments. Some they had read about in advertisements for the Swears and Wells store's wintertime sales. By the time they stepped off the bus in Castle Bailey Street, they were all excited by the prospect of their shopping trip. None of them realised then that this would be their last sight of the crowded shops that graced the middle of the town centre.

Norma, who now lives in Sketty, recalls how she had just finished her shopping and that she and her friends were clutching their carrier bags and chatting. She remembers how they were trying to decide whether to have a last-minute cup of tea in one of the many High Street cafés, even though they were just as eager to get home to try on their new purchases. Finally, they decided it was better to go home. Norma had just turned towards Castle Street and started to walk in the direction of the bus stop:

> Suddenly, I stopped in my tracks to see people running in all directions down each of the side streets as well as back up the High Street. Others were running down the steep slope of Welcome Lane, which leads towards the Strand and away from the vicinity of Castle Street. But, even as I stood recovering from the feeling of stunned disbelief, and started to run in the direction of the Square, I could hear voices shouting: 'Run, run. Unexploded bomb!'

Norma describes how within a few minutes they were surrounded by dozens of uniformed firefighters, police and ARP officers, who seemed to appear from every direction. They were waving their arms frantically and shouting directions to the public as well as to each other. Then, before Norma and the people around her could react to the warning, there was a massive, earth-moving explosion. It was only later she discovered that this was the moment when the Castle Street bomb exploded and the young bomb-disposal team were killed. The impact from the blast threw her off her feet and she landed face down on the ground. She had cut her lip, yet, even then, as she tried to struggle to her feet, she considered herself lucky to be alive. Looking about, she said, there were many people lying on the ground, or else sitting up with obviously broken bones and bleeding limbs: 'In spite of my own state, the sight of the others made me realise that I had miraculously managed to escape from injuries that could have been far worse.'

It was only when Norma finally stood up and started feeling dizzy that she found shrapnel and debris from the explosion had hit her on the back of her head. Through the chaos and cries going on around her, Norma felt someone stop and help her walk towards the first-aid post. As far as she can recall, the post stood on the corner of the narrow, cobbled lane which once ran alongside the Lewis Lewis department store in High Street, and led to Orchard Street and the side of the police station building. When she reached the first-aid post, she was treated by the nursing aids for her head injuries as well as cuts and bruises. These aids were among the large number of people of all ages who had volunteered to give up their time to help with the nursing care, even at the height of the blitz. Then, after she was given a welcome cup of tea, she was allowed to leave. Back at home, she discovered her parents' St Thomas house had been hit by an incendiary bomb. After a few days' extra leave to recover, she returned to her nursing duties. Then, as the war continued, she gave up her nursing job. Norma joined the hundreds who volunteered for the Swansea Fire Service. There, under the direction of her boss Mr May, then the head of the Fire Service, she helped to serve food and also with first-aid duties. Later, she returned to work as a nurse, at the Cefn Coed Hospital in Swansea.

CHAPTER SEVEN

Irene Coles

Irene Coles, 2006. (Courtesy Irene Coles)

At the time of the blitz, Irene Coles was living with her parents in St Thomas. After she left school, she spent many years working in the Castle Cinema as a cashier. Throughout the war years, people still queued for their weekly night out at the pictures. She says that, in spite of the constant threat of air raids and the disruption to transport, the cinema was still filled to capacity every night. It was as if people were determined to carry on as normally as possible in spite of the war. For many people at that time, it was a case of feeling there was a kind of security in being together. Others found it a great comfort to be able to get away from the horrors of war. It was also a common belief that escaping, even for a few hours, might help them to cope better. On screen, the films reflected the mood of heroism and adventure. One of them was the story of *Stanley and Livingstone*, which starred Spencer Tracy. The wartime tickets for the best seats, which were in the circle, cost around three shillings. Otherwise, cinema-goers, called 'patrons', paid ninepence for the cheap seats in the back row. Irene remembers the first night of the blitz:

As usual, I was working in my ticket kiosk in the foyer of the cinema. I also took my turn at selling the ices during the intervals. We were about halfway through the evening's programme when we heard the air-raid siren warning the blitz was about to begin. Then the bombing started. Firstly, the sound was in the distance and drawing closer by the minute. At one time, the whole place shuddered and you could hear the planes overhead and the air raids going on outside.

However, in spite of the notice that came up on the screen telling people that they could leave the cinema if they wished to do so, most of them stayed in their seats until the end of the film. After the bombing raid was over and the all-clear sounded, I went outside to Castle Street. I could not believe what had happened. When I looked towards Kilvey Hill, I could see it lit up by incendiary bombs. There were fires and ambulances everywhere you looked, and the smell of burning and thick smoke in the air. I kept tripping up over the rubble. People around me were shouting and crying. When I looked around, the old castle did not look too bad. In fact, I remember seeing it silhouetted and thinking well, it does not look so bad. Well, it was not, compared with the rest of the town. Castle Street and the surrounding area was lit up in a bright red glow. The lovely Ben Evans store where I had shopped ever since I was a girl was ablaze. Through the smoke, all you could see was the outline of the building. The Three Lamps Hotel that stood opposite the cinema and Edward the Eagle shop was on fire too. The noise was almost deafening. Buildings were falling down and the firefighters and hoses were everywhere.

There must have been hundreds of people in the cinema that night but, as far as I can remember, we all managed to get out of there safely. At least, there were no reports of any casualties. On the following night, the bombing raids were even worse. More buildings disappeared. I could not even begin to

Part of the Castle Cinema where Irene Coles worked as a cashier during the nights of the blitz. Considering how close the cinema was to the scene of the blitz, it was a miracle the building survived.

describe the terrible sight of the old market building, which had been part of the town for so many years. That had been bombed out of recognition. The glass from the market roof was everywhere you looked. David Evans store was ablaze and the lovely old St Mary's Church was nothing but an empty shell in the middle of the ruins of Caer Street, Goat Street and the surrounding acres of rubble. The Swansea of my childhood had been such a lovely, happy place to live. I felt sad when I realised it had gone for good.

At the start of the war, the women's contribution to the war effort was mainly voluntary. By late 1940, National Service became compulsory for unmarried women aged between 20 and 30 and in 1943 the age group rose to include women up to 50, unless they were mothers of children under 14 years old. For Irene, a single woman, it meant leaving her cinema job and working as an acetylene welder in the munitions factory. She was sad. Working in the cinema was a job she had done for many years, and a job she had loved. Yet, as she says, in those days you knuckled down to things and got on with it. You told yourself there were always many others who were far worse off than you were.

CHAPTER EIGHT

Haydn Jack Thomas

A young Haydn Thomas. (Courtesy Haydn Thomas)

The Three Nights' Blitz on Swansea caused the most widespread devastation the town had ever known. There were also many other long and sustained bombing raids on parts of the town during the early years of the war. One of the first of these raids came without warning at 3.30 a.m. on a night in June 1940, when the bombers dropped several high-explosive bombs on Kilvey Hill, although four of the bombs, reportedly, failed to explode. The bombers continued with their raids and caused numerous deaths and much destruction to the residential areas of Danygraig, St Thomas and Port Tennant, as well as the dockside nearby.

Haydn Jack Thomas, from Sketty, had left school by the time the Second World War began. He remembers the horror he felt at seeing the devastation of the St Thomas area that he and his family had known for decades as home, and the disruption to family and working life caused by the bombing.

As a boy, Haydn grew up at 22 Benthall Place, St Thomas, where he lived with his family. He remembers how the house stood facing the Morris Lane Church

The former Morris Lane Church School. The building no longer exists, but it was an important part of the war effort. Haydn recalls how it was used by the RAF Air Sea Rescue unit.

School – the school building is no longer there. He recalls how, at the time of the Three Nights' Blitz, he had found employment in a shop as an errand boy. Mr Watts the shop owner was Haydn's boss, and he recalls how the shop was described as a 'high-class shipping grocer'. It was situated on the corner of the Fabian Way, that stood between Miers Street and Inkerman Street long before the familiar streets disappeared and became part of the vast modern-day landscape. Haydn recalls how much enthusiasm he had for his first job and how he could not wait to turn up each morning for work.

As an errand lad, I would cycle to deliver the goods to the houses. In those days, St Thomas was full of long, narrow streets lined with terraced houses, a variety of shops and friendly people. The customers who came to buy at the shop were sometimes what we called 'well-to-do'. That meant they were rich and used to a first-class delivery service that Mr Watts and I kept aiming for.

So, every morning, I would turn up early for work. I rode one of those old-style bikes with upright handlebars that we called 'sit up and beg'. There was a metal basket in front of the bike that was made to carry the groceries I delivered on my rounds. Quite often I filled the basket of customers' groceries so full that I found myself cycling around corners of the streets with my back wheel raised in the air.

Haydn also recalls the time he will never forget and the devastation and misery that thousands like him experienced during the three nights of the blitz. 'Just looking at the remains of the damaged buildings, and the town centre of which Swansea residents had been so proud, was heartbreaking.' He also remembers the morning after the blitz, when Mr Watts called at his home. Together, Haydn and his boss walked towards Fabian Way already fearing what the bombers had done to the shop as well as their livelihoods. Their foreboding proved to be right. When they reached the area, they could see the shop had been bombed on the night before. Like the surrounding streets that Haydn had known for most of his life, the shop had disappeared beneath a huge mountain of debris and craters. Naturally, Mr Watts was devastated and never had the heart to open a shop again. Likewise, Haydn's job as an errand boy ended too, but the war went on.

The evacuation of children from the danger areas meant that Haydn and his sister Dorothy moved to Brynamman, a good 10 miles north of Swansea. Their parents believed the children would be safer and would soon settle down in the countryside. However, both Haydn and Dorothy had other ideas. They were determined not to stay away from their home for long. Between them, they thought up a plan to escape. Without telling anyone, they decided to take the bus back home to Swansea. Naturally, given the circumstances, they had no money. They managed to persuade the bus conductor to take down their names and address, and they did finally return home from Brynamman. Thankfully, their parents were happy to see them, but they were less pleased to discover that their children had dared to travel so far on their own.

Over the years since the war, Haydn has often looked back to the past and thought about the area of his childhood home. He is surprised to find that no wartime records seem to exist as to the significance of the Morris Lane Church School, that is, the part it played in the war effort. Haydn recalls a time at the start of the war years when he learned how the RAF Air Sea Rescue unit took over the Morris Lane school building, as well as the house at 22 Benthall Place where he had once lived. He further recalls that the house at No. 23, next door, was also requisitioned. It was used as the headquarters for the officers and personnel of the District RAF. By that time, Haydn had joined the Army Cadet Force, which he thinks was known as the 14th Glamorgan Unit. He says, 'We used to use J Shed on the Swansea Docks as a rifle range.' Alas, the wartime J Shed, like many of the old buildings, today has become lost amid the changing landscape of the modern city.

CHAPTER NINE

Peggie Lowe

Peggie Lowe served the favourite drink of cocoa during her days in the NAAFI. (Courtesy Peggie Lowe)

Its close proximity to the BP oil refinery at Llandarcy made Swansea Docks and the surrounding areas the most obvious target for enemy action. In what is regarded as the first large air raid to take place in September 1940, the Llandarcy oil refinery was set ablaze. Peggie Lowe from Skewen was a young woman of 24 when the war began. She was working as a steel erector's mate at the Llandarcy oil refinery and remembers how the bombs fell regularly in the dock area, as well as on the different parts of the town. Yet she went on working along with her wartime workmates. Mostly, these were women in their thirties, either married or single, and there was a comradeship among them all. Like Peggie, despite the dangers around them they all believed it was a matter of getting on with it and not letting things get you down. Part of Peggie's job meant that she spent hours on end painting sheds and buildings with red lead. Many of her colleagues worked as fitter's mates, while others were given the task of filling jerrycans with petrol to store for the use of wartime vehicles. Peggie regularly faced the challenge of joining other steel erectors to make a few 'minor' repairs. This meant they climbed nearly 70ft into the air. There she stood with her two feet balanced on two small wooden planks. Then it was time for her to start repairing the bomb-damaged glass skylights that were set in the roofs of the works sheds.

However, it was only after the war that Peggie discovered what had been her most significant wartime task, when she found to her surprise that she had become involved in the activities of PLUTO, which played a crucial role in the success of the Allied offensive after D-Day. PLUTO was the wartime code name that was given to the Pipeline under the Ocean. This was a pipe laid underneath the sea that would eventually supply fuel from England to the Allied troops in Europe to keep their vehicles moving. The pipe was partly constructed, and tested in secret, in a small shed in Peggie's workplace. The first operational test was actually carried out between Swansea and Ilfracombe, across the Bristol Channel.

One day, her boss called Peggie and her mate into the main office. The two women workers were given details of a job they were to undertake. It transpired that the task was to be carried out in a small shed that was down at the docks. On the way, she and her mate were sworn to secrecy regarding the job itself, as well as the shed's location. They were told that a pump was to be built for the purpose of training the soldiers to pump oil beneath the sea. Peggie recalls that neither she nor her mate had any idea of the significance of the task at the time. 'All we knew was that the wartime service personnel who operated the pump needed an adequate shed to protect the pump from the wet weather.' Thus Peggie and her mate found that their special job was to paint the shed with red lead. When it was complete, the whole area was camouflaged. Even years after the war, Peggie found it hard to realise how important that little dockside shed would become, or that she would ever have found herself, even in the smallest way, becoming involved in the preparations for the PLUTO D-Day success.

As the war years continued, Peggie volunteered for duties in the NAAFI, the Navy, Army and Air Force Institution. Her duties were looking after the serving

Peggie Lowe, 2006.

soldiers who were stationed at the Old Guildhall. She knew that, although the NAAFI volunteers wore uniforms, working here was not considered a compulsory task. As Peggie explains, 'You could leave at any time, in theory, but not many of us did. We were pleased to be part of the war effort. My job was to serve the teas to the service men and women. The favourite day was Friday when the 'boys' came to buy their rations of sweets and cigarettes.'

During the Swansea Blitz, Peggie was working as a supervisor at Hope Brothers, one of the men's tailor's shops in the High Street. She also held the distinction of being one of the first women to be employed in what was known then as a male domain. Throughout the blitz, she continued to walk the 8- mile journey from her home in Skewen to work and back. She puts it very starkly: 'Even after the bombings of the night before, the shop workers were still expected to turn up for work the next day. Only, before we could start, we had to clear up the damage the bombers had caused to the shop.'

Peggie was also among the many shop assistants and other workers who regularly paused in their work duties to step outside to the High Street to help the workers on the streets. These were the men sent into town to clear up the sites that had been blasted by the bombers; or else they were there to detect and sometimes defuse the unexploded bombs that still lay buried all over town. Peggie was there to serve them cups of cocoa, their favourite drink. She did this several times a day, but, as she recalls, there was one day that she has never forgotten. 'As usual, I went into the High Street to hand the group of young men their drinks. We stood together laughing for a few minutes, before I turned back to the shop. Minutes later, the whole place shook as an unexploded bomb went off. All the men I had spoken to minutes earlier were dead.'

CHAPTER TEN

Michael Hart

Mike Hart, third from left, known as 'The Joker' to his fellow Royal Engineers, c. 1942.
(Courtesy Mike Hart)

Mike Hart, 2006.

Michael Hart, from Sketty, lived in Greenhill during the war. He owned a shop which stood on the corner of Caerpystill Street and Llangyfelach Street. He recalls how the shop was typical of the corner shops of the time. Up until the wartime rationing shortages, it 'sold everything'. Mike says he saw out most of the days of the Second World War in the Royal Engineers, and took part in the D-Day landings. He recalls one time when he was injured and was sent back home to spend time as a patient in Cefn Coed Hospital. During the war, the hospital included wards reserved for servicemen.

CHAPTER ELEVEN

John Madge

John Madge as a young boy outside his aunt's house, where he stayed during the blitz. (Courtesy John Madge)

John Madge, 2006. (Courtesy John Madge)

John Madge lives in Llansamlet. He was a small boy at the start of the Second World War and has clear memories of the Swansea Blitz. On the first night of the bombing raids he was sitting with his mother at their home in Gwynedd Avenue. After they had made their way to the air-raid shelter, they sat listening to the bombs falling around them. John says he heard later that some of the bombers had missed their target. Instead of dropping on the docks, the incendiaries fell across the steep heights of Kilvey Hill, a well-known landmark that rose over the town. Many people described the blazing hill as 'an awesome sight', like 'one big candle-lit cake'. It was visible great distances away from the town. As John recalls, 'Naturally, my mother and I were terrified.'

On the following day, his mother decided that they were going to stay with her sister, John's aunt Dolly, Dorothy Blanchett, who lived in nearby Hill Terrace Road. On the second night of the blitz, John recalls, the air-raid warning sirens started earlier than they had done the night before. As John and his mother sat in his aunt's house, they could hear the whine of the bombs falling and feel the impact from the blast as they hit the ground. The three of them sat huddled underneath the staircase, listening to the sound becoming louder. They could feel the floor shaking beneath them as the bombers were getting closer. Suddenly, there was one massive, almost deafening explosion. John remembers how he could feel the floors and ceilings of the house shuddering so much that it was hard to stand up and keep his balance.

Then cracking sounds started all around them. They all thought that the walls were going to cave in and the house was about to fall on top of them. From the street outside came the sound of pandemonium. John could hear people screaming and shouting at each other. There was also the sound of fire engines and ambulances in the distance. After he, his mother and his aunt had sat waiting for a time that seemed like hours, everything seemed to stop. There were a few more moments of silence. Then they heard the sound of the siren giving the all-clear.

Finally, John's aunt and his mother gathered their coats and their belongings together. With some difficulty, they managed to open the front door. John could smell the smoke and hear the crackle of flames from the burning buildings nearby. The air was full of grey smoke and bits of flying debris as well as soot out of the chimneys from the open coal fires that most people had then. He also remembers how they had to step their way between piles of bricks and stones as they went into the street to observe the damage. Even then, they all stood together looking about them, numbed with disbelief.

John could see an enormous crater had appeared just a few paces from the house where they had all clung together moments earlier. They could also see that just a few steps further down the street, the bombers had scored a direct hit on St Jude's Church. The bomb blast had also thrown a huge mound of earth against the walls of a house on the other side of Hill Terrace Road. Mr and Mrs Jones, the house's occupants, considered themselves lucky, although they had to spend the rest of the week trying to dig a path out of their own gateway. John recalls how they too considered themselves lucky because, despite how close they had been to the falling bombs, they had survived. He was also amazed to find that only one small window was broken in his Aunt Dolly's house.

As the war continued, John was like most of the small boys who lived through the bombing raids. There were parts of it he found exciting, such as collecting the pieces of shrapnel after the raids. He recalls:

Our home in Gwynedd Avenue had an air-raid shelter in the back garden. This is where we sat whenever there was a particularly heavy air raid taking place. I sat listening to the sound of the scattering of shrapnel on the roof of the shelter and along our garden path. I could also hear the sound of the anti-aircraft guns that seemed to fire regularly over the nearby Cockett area. Each morning, after the raids, we boys would hurry out to our class in Gorse Road Junior School. There we would stand in the playground and compare the various pieces that we had found the night before. The bigger the piece, the better we liked it.

John remembers how the wartime school activities also involved him in plane spotting:

It was in the early years of the war. We school pupils were standing out in the schoolyard during the morning break. Suddenly we heard the sound of a fighter plane in the distance. People told us how to tell the sound of the

John Madge with his cousin, Joan Madge. (Courtesy John Madge)

different warplanes. The German planes had a distinct sound of a diesel whine to them. We could also tell by the purring sound that it was a British plane. So we knew by the sound that this particular plane was different. As it flew nearer, we could see to our delight that it was a Spitfire. We knew the 'Spit' by the sound as well as the look that we thought was unique. The plane also had a sharklike way of flying, slightly nose down, unlike any other aircraft we had seen. We schoolkids stood cheering and waving. We were wild with excitement and even more delighted when the pilot spotted us and waved back. Then the pilot turned the plane into a low swoop before passing over the school playground. Finally, the plane came so low that we could see the pilot clearly. As you can guess, the sight of one of our boys showing us he was not afraid of anything . . . It was the main topic of our school-day conversation for weeks afterwards.

CHAPTER TWELVE

Olive Gray

Olive Gray in her NAAFI uniform, August 1941. (Courtesy Olive Gray)

Olive Gray lives in St Thomas. During the blitz, she was working in the centre of town. She considers that compared with many people she was very lucky, as she experienced 'quite a few near misses' during the nights of the bombing raids. At the time, she was 20 years old and worked as one of the waiting staff at the Royal Hotel, which was at the top of High Street. She says she was happy working there and that she had many friends. One of the highlights of the week was getting together and going to the cinema or the dance halls, and walking along Oxford Street, a lively part of the town:

> You could always tell what night it was by the groups of young people enjoying their weekly night out. For example, every Thursday was when the shop assistants got together for a night at the cinema. Friday was when every kind of worker was out at the dance halls or the pictures. Then came Saturday, the traditional night when all the office staff dressed up for the night out at a restaurant or the ballroom.

Before the Three Nights' Blitz, Olive recalls there had been a few smaller raids at night, which as far as she could tell caused no major damage. There were also daytime raids, mainly over the docks. She says they could never have imagined that the worst ordeals were still to come. On the first night of the blitz, all the customers from the hotel went home. That left Olive, the cook and the chambermaid. As the bar was open, the three of them worked there until she prepared to lay the table for some special guests, twenty fire officers who had travelled from London. Then, just as they had finished their meal and remarked on the 'lovely moonlit night', bombs started falling in what looked like snow drifting down from the skies. Olive continues, 'I was outside the hotel watching the unforgettable sight as the bombs fell onto Ben Evans store. At the same time, one of my duties during the raids was to supply the ARP and other workers with food and hot drinks. One night, one of these men, a Mr Thomas, came into the hotel and reported that everything was all right.'

Olive begged him to stay and have a cup of tea, but he refused, saying he would call back as he wanted to go to the Wesley Chapel air-raid shelter to check that everyone was all right. That was the night that the chapel took a direct hit during the bombing raid, and he never returned. Only his tin helmet was recovered, a fitting tribute and a reminder that the ARP thought only of others.

The bombing went on and Olive recalls that she could be with people one minute, while the next they were blown away. She talks about 'having nine lives' given the way she managed to escape serious injuries; particularly as she goes on to describe how, as the blitz continued, the bombs hit the hotel and killed several people who were standing outside. While none of the hotel staff were hurt, the damage to the High Street and as far as the railway station was 'shocking'. She recalls that by then the time was almost midnight and her boss, who was also the Head Warden, came and ordered her to leave the hotel and get into the nearest air-raid shelter, which was in the Strand:

Olive Gray, 2006. (Courtesy Olive Gray)

On the way, I took an injured lad and two serving officers with me, as they could not get to the docks. This is because so much damage had been done to the town centre and the area around Wind Street, St Thomas and the Docks. Eventually, we managed to pick our way through the rubble. I was just about getting into the shelter and shutting the door when a land mine whizzed past me and fell in the Hafod area. At 3 a.m. on the Saturday morning, my boss came to look for me. Strangely, I was concerned that I did not look a happy sight as I was still dressed in my waiting clothes, and my apron was dirty.

Finally, the all-clear came at last. The devastation of the town was heartbreaking. The bombers had flattened all the Castle Street and High Street shops that we had known all our lives. No one had a job. But, after a while, such was the spirit of the people in the town, Swansea soon got moving again, finding new business premises. Staff and bosses alike rolled up their sleeves and, by Monday morning, the shops left were doing business again. Then we went to Oxford Street, to find it was not there anymore. The market was a heap of rubble and glass, the shops had gone and the damage to the lovely St Mary's Church was unbelievable. People stood silent and too shocked to cry. There was no Swansea anymore. I lost my job, as the hotel was badly damaged. Yet I still consider myself as lucky to come out alive.

Later, at the age of 21, Olive says, 'I got my calling-up papers and was placed in the NAAFI,' although she admits it was not quite by choice, but because of her catering experience. She spent the next four years with the NAAFI being stationed in different parts of Wales. She recalls, 'The work was hard and the hours were long but the workforce lived by the motto: "We serve those who serve." The serving officers often made fun of us, but we felt quite smart in our NAAFI uniforms.'

After she was promoted to manager, Olive found the work was even more demanding. The morning began by making the tea in an urn that took twenty cups of tea to each gallon of water. Then there were times when taking the teas to the aerodrome with the almost gale-force winds caused the tea wagon to nearly turn over. There was no time to worry when they knew the 'boys' were waiting for their precious cups of tea and a bun. Many of the boys were homesick, and they would ask the girls to write to them, although Olive recalls there were happy times too. Dances and variety shows were regularly held at the camps or outside. By 1942, Olive was married and was lucky enough to be transferred with her husband to the same camp in Rhyl, North Wales. In spite of everything, everyone made the best of things, she says. 'I always had the satisfaction of knowing that what I was doing was worthwhile.'

CHAPTER THIRTEEN

Jack Miller

Jack Miller (left) with his friend Glyn Ferris, 1946. Glyn lived at Walter Street, Manselton, and was best man at Miller's wedding in 1951. His mother had a shop in Elgin Street. Later Glyn ran two shops in Swansea; one at Alexander Road near Ralph's, a well-known local bookshop, and one in Wind Street near Salubrious Passage.
(Courtesy Jack Miller)

Jack Miller lives with his wife Beryl in Landore. He was a school pupil of 14 years old at the start of the war. He recalls the day when, as he made his way to the Swansea Grammar School on the morning of the blitz, he could not have imagined that this would be the last time he would be able to recognise the town centre. At the time, he was living with his parents in Monterey Street, Manselton. On that first night, when the bombing raids began, he and his friend were standing in the doorway of a chip shop in Eaton Road. As Jack recalled, the boys had just left the shop clutching their wrapped-up meals and were half-way across Eaton Road and heading towards Bohun Street. All of a sudden, he heard a loud bang and the ground shook beneath them. At the same time, the boys looked up to see what appeared to be huge snowflakes falling all around them and covering the ground. Then, Jack heard the sound of the air-raid warning, which, people said later, went off at about 7.50 p.m.

Naturally, Jack and his friend did not stop to take notice of the time. The two of them ran from the road, along the Manselton streets and into his friend's house. For a long time, they sat together in the living room and listening to the drone of the planes as the bombers flew backwards and forwards across the town centre and beyond. At the same time, Jack recalls, 'We could hear the fizzing sound of the incendiary bombs that started to fall outside and onto the pavements and the garden paths. Or else they thudded against the side of the house. Then, before long, the high-explosive bombs were falling all around us. All any of us could do was sit through it all and wait for what seemed like hours for the sound of the all-clear.'

On the second night of the blitz, the bombing raids were even worse. It was the night when the air raids caused damage to Jack's house, when the bombs fell on Bohun Street and Manor Road in the Manselton area.

In July 1942, Jack left school at the age of 16 and began work on the railway, which he continued throughout the years of the war. As a junior GWR employee, he began his work as an engine cleaner at the Landore locomotive shed. This was the first step to a footplate career, and Jack's ambition was to follow the same progress as his father Len and become an engine driver. From his initial training he moved on to help out in the shed office. There, his duties as a time clerk meant that he did shift work at the Neath locomotive shed. The shed had a carriage and wagon repair shop attached. Jack recalls how the trains were kept running regularly throughout the war despite the many wartime restrictions and the constant threat of air raids.

During the evening, night-time and weekends, one of Jack's wartime duties was to take telephone messages to the superintendent's office at Cadoxton, Neath:

The messages included a large number of code words. But, naturally, the details of any movement or destination of the troop and ammunition trains were kept secret. Such messages were always sent to the Stationmaster in sealed envelopes. Railway staff were instructed to go and meet the trains at certain times and to receive the envelopes from the passenger train guard.

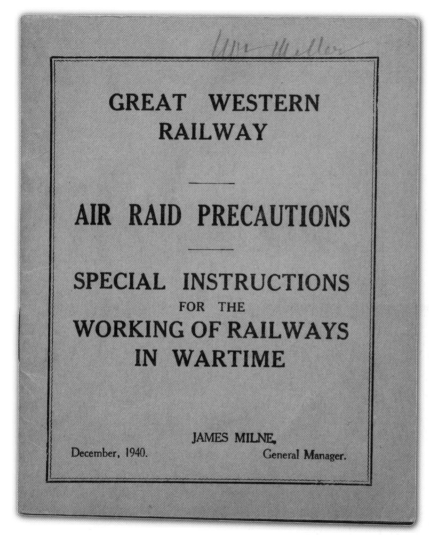

A GWR Air-Raid Precautions booklet, explaining the Air-Raid Warning Systems, issued in 1940 to Jack Miller's father, Len. (Courtesy Jack Miller)

Jack himself met a number of these trains at the Landore station to receive the sealed envelopes, which he handed to the head foreman.

At the times when the public air-raid warning siren sounded, Jack would work for a number of hours by the only light, which came from an oil lamp in the railway office. There was also great difficulty when it came to people finding their way around. This is because all direction and destination signs were removed from the stations. Naturally, the rules for the railway staff and the train passengers were strict. Some of these wartime rules are seen in the *GWR Air-Raid Precautions*, a booklet that was issued to Jack's father Len in 1940. At the time, such information was confidential. It explains the air-raid warning systems and the rules for passenger and railway personnel travelling on the trains.

CHAPTER FOURTEEN

Sadie Lewis and Rebecca Waters

The author's mother Sadie Lewis, right, with Mrs 'Mac' Davies, a baker who lived in Cross Street. Mrs Davies never failed to deliver the daily bread throughout the war. She was a friend and confidante to the Lewis family and their neighbours on her Brynhyfryd baker's round.

The author's mother, Sadie Lewis, and her aunt, Rebecca Waters (known to her friends as Becca), were brought up in Brynhyfryd. Becca often described to the author what Swansea was like before the blitz. She talked about the time when the daily milk, loaves of bread and paraffin for heaters, and in some areas household coal, were delivered by horse and cart. There were also the big shire horses that looked as if they were made especially for pulling the brewery carriages. These were the huge wagons filled with barrels of beer which the breweries used for their regular deliveries to the local public houses. 'I used to love their colourful presence and the sound of their clattering hooves on the road,' said Becca. 'I also loved the sound of the barrels rolling down the cellars of the Morris Arms, a well-known public house which stood opposite the house where we lived in Llangyfelach Road.'

In town, just opposite the High Street railway station, was the Mackworth Hotel. This was a grand place with a wide staircase and a dark red interior. People who travelled to Swansea from miles around would not miss the chance to shop at the renowned Lewis Lewis department store. The customers, well used to the double Lewis name, always sat waiting patiently their turn for the attention of the shop assistants. This was often to buy the then-popular fashion of two-piece suits, which were known as 'costumes' in the department the clothiers called 'gowns and mantles'. The drapery department sold fabric from the dress designs that customers could view on the plaster mannequins in the shop's window display. Customers from that era also recall how the cash bells hung on overhead wires and criss-crossed the ceiling of the store. Even during wartime, the strict department-store rules remained. Thus, no matter what the situation, the policy at most stores was 'the customer is always right', and woe betide anyone who dared to flout it. The words 'Can I help you, madam?' were meant to be for the benefit of the customer, and when it came to the arrangement of the pre-war department store, the customer's comfort was also a major consideration. There were chairs set at every counter, and every purchase was met with the shop assistant's personal service and professional smile. It sounds good, but shopping for fashion could mean hours in the fitting room. It meant other customers had to sit patiently waiting their turn in the queue. The whole experience took a long time.

In contrast there was the quick shopping service of Woolworth's where, Becca said:

Everyone found a way to make sure our young life went on normally, even during the war. We girls went shopping for Woollies' earrings and bought make-up to go with our latest powder compacts. We also loved the Phulnana scent that we dabbed behind our ears. We also bought stockings made from lisle as none of us had heard of nylons at that time. Regularly, we went to the Castle, the Albert Hall or the Plaza Cinema to see our favourite film stars, Spencer Tracy, Greer Garson or Jean Simmons. There were dances we went to that were held in most of the church halls, although these were tame affairs, with strict rules of behaviour, compared with that of the later generation of teenagers and rock and roll.

Throughout the blitz and the war years, we still carried on with our young lives in the best way we could. Mostly, we found getting home in the blackout was a problem due to the blackout and traffic restrictions. Understandably, the bus times were unpredictable and most of the time the drivers refused, or else were only able to go so far because of the bomb damage, or the warning signs. Even on foot, you were lucky if you could avoid the hazards of further roadblocks caused by rubble or fire officers' hose pipes. You were just as likely to come across [a] warning sign to keep back from the danger of bomb-damaged buildings falling down or the fear of unexploded bombs.

On the other hand, as we were all in the same boat, there was always a camaraderie among us. Strangers linked arms and grouped together sharing our wartime experiences and jokes. One of my friends told me how she had walked into a horse tied to a post during the blackout. She said her screams had scared the poor animal more than the sound of the bombs. However, as most of us had sweethearts or relatives serving overseas, there were the bad times, too. Secretly, we all lived in dread of the sight of the boy on the bike who delivered the telegrams. The minute you saw him approach the front door, you knew deep in your heart that it meant bad news. You were likely to read the encrypted telegram message that informed you a loved one was dead, or else missing in action. Lovers at home were also parted. As the bombing in Swansea continued, I sat with many of my friends grieving for their loved ones.

One night, my father James Waters, told me how he nearly lost his life, but for what must have been one of the luckier stories of the war. He recounted how he was walking to his home that stood opposite the Morris Arms public house on the night of the Brynhyfryd bombing blast. He had almost reached the house in Llangyfelach Road when the braces he used to keep his trousers up broke suddenly. He had just stopped in his tracks to adjust the braces, when the sudden blast threw him forward onto his knees. As the carnage continued around him, he yelled back at the enemy. Then he went on kneeling in the middle of the pavement, with his hands covering his head. After the air raid was over, he continued on his way and found the front door of our home splintered by the impact of the bombs. For many years afterwards, he recalled how lucky he had been that he had been prevented from going on his way.

Becca continued:

At the time of the blast, I was at our neighbour's air-raid shelter with my sister Sadie and her baby, my niece Sally [the author]. Our elderly neighbour was keeping watch outside and muttering something like 'There goes the chapel . . . there goes Penfilia . . .

When the all-clear siren sounded and we climbed out of the shelter, we saw our faces were blackened with coal dust and our knees felt like jelly. 'That's it for tonight,' someone said, then we laughed, mainly through our terror and relief that we were still alive. Yet we believed that things would get worse before it got better.

AUGUST 1940

One Saturday in August 1940, more than thirty high-explosive bombs were dropped over Swansea during a heavy midnight air raid. The bombs caused damage to the railway viaduct at Landore, and to hundreds of houses and businesses in the surrounding areas of Cwmbwrla, Manselton and Brynhyfryd. Sadie Lewis and her baby daughter Sally were living in Llangyfelach Road, Brynhyfryd, Sadie's childhood home. Her husband Ken was away in the army. Sadie remembered the night when high-explosive bombs fell directly on nearby Landore, Manselton and Penfilia, and Brynhyfryd took the impact from the blasts.

In those days Sadie, like most people, was too afraid to go upstairs to bed because of the danger of bombs hitting the roof. Sadie was sitting with her baby, wrapped up in a shawl, huddled in the living room with her sister Becca. She recalled how they heard the bombs starting to fall. Within minutes they both realised there was no time to get to the air-raid shelter, although it was only two doors away in a neighbour's garden. They sat in the house as the bombing took hold. Then there was an almost deafening crash as the front door splintered into pieces. At the same time coal, soot and sparks from the open fire in the hearth scattered dirt, dust and smut around the living-room. In the chaos, Sadie grabbed her baby from the makeshift cot on the settee and pushed her into a cupboard beneath the stairs.

Back in the living room, Sadie and Becca clung together as the bombing continued, until finally the all-clear siren told them the raid was over and Sadie retrieved the baby from the cupboard. All their faces and clothes and everything in the room had been blackened by the flying debris. In spite of all the horror, Sadie had to laugh. Apart from what had happened to the front door, the flying soot had caused more damage to the house than the bombers had done. Within hours the Llangyfelach Road neighbours arrived armed with brushes, dusters and mops to help clear up the mess. Sadie was more than grateful for such neighbourly help. She also realised how lucky they had been to survive.

BOMB BLASTS AND DANCING SHOES

Although Becca worked mainly in London, she regularly came home to Brynhyfryd to stay with her sister and experienced the effects of the London bombing as well as the Swansea Blitz. Becca remembered that on one occasion as her train approached Swansea she heard the sound of the air-raid warning. The train stopped a long way short of the platform at High Street railway station. She was told that the bombs had dropped on the town centre and the passengers had to stay put in the carriage until they heard the sound of the all-clear:

Rebecca 'Becca' Waters, the author's aunt, who was born and grew up in Swansea during the war years.

Naturally, everyone was worried sick about their loved ones who lived in the town. It was obvious something bad had happened. But, at the same time, there was nothing that any of us could do but wait. By the time the train finally managed to arrive at the station, all that could be seen of the town was a red glow over the sky, and the smell of acrid smoke was thick in the air.

Nothing in the world prepared me for the sights as I left the station and walked down High Street towards Castle Street. I could hardly recognise what was left of my home town. All I could see was heaps of stone, rubble wood and glass. There were fire hoses, shouting, dazed people walking about and

The author's childhood home, one of the row of terraced houses in Llangyfelach Road, which took the impact of the wartime bombing raids. The VE celebrations took place in nearby Eaton Road.

ambulances everywhere you looked. Someone said the Wesley Chapel had 'gone up'. A woman helped off a bus fell onto the pavement in a dead faint. I found out that her husband had been reported as one of the hundreds of people killed by the bombs. I walked back to the station and onto Brynhyfryd, so relieved to find my family, and our home, but for the front door, was still intact.

When not in London, Becca worked as an assistant in the Kardomah Café, as well as a volunteer with the Red Cross. The volunteers operated from first-aid posts that were situated all over town. She said:

We treated minor injuries, of course, but we also handed out cups of tea and tried our best to comfort those who were bereaved, and those made homeless by the bombers. After the air raids, you could smell cordite and burning in the air for days afterwards. A pall of grey dust also seemed to linger over the town. Although it was night, and the blackout regulations were in force, the whole town was lit up like daylight by the parachute flares. That made it easy for the Luftwaffe to view the area for miles around. You could see the fires burning as far as Kilvey Hill. However, for most people the attitude was 'just go on as best you can'.

Becca, top right, and friends. Becca is dressed in the 'latest' pre-war fashion.

Becca, front row, left, with a group of her work colleagues.

The author's late parents Sadie and Ken, right, with Sadie's brother Bill, centre, and his wife Sue left.

Becca went on to recall how the war

certainly did not stop the single girls like us making the most of our time off. There were always the cinemas and the dance halls such as the Patti – particularly when the Americans arrived in town.

While we girls taught them the old-time steps, they taught everyone to do the jitterbug. Another time, we had just heard the air-raid warning, and I remembered I had left my new dance shoes in a café in Union Street. I wanted to go back and fetch them and created such a fuss when the fire officers stopped me going back into the streets in that part of town. The next morning, I found out why. The bombs from the air raid the night before had demolished the market and Saint Mary's Church. The bombs had also destroyed buildings in Oxford Street, Union Street and Park Street. It is where, had I returned to the café, I might have become one of the large number of casualties. Amazingly, although anyone would say it was typical of the Swansea people's pride and spirit, even those whose homes had been damaged returned to their workplace on the following days after the blitz to help to clear up the mess. It was hard for anyone to realise that all the shops that had made up the town centre had disappeared for good.

Becca Waters in later years. During the war she worked in London and regularly returned home to Swansea.

The author's neighbours were the stalwarts of Llangyfelach Road during the war and long afterwards. From left to right: Nancy Bristow, the author's father and Iris John.

St Joseph's Church, now a cathedral, where Becca Waters shared her friends' wartime grief.

Aftermath of the Oxford Street bombing which destroyed a row of shops and the glass-covered market (to the left of the buses). (Courtesy South Wales Evening Post)

CHAPTER FIFTEEN

Bernard Evans

Bernard and his sister Glenys Sanders, more than sixty years after the war.
(Courtesy Bernard Evans)

Swansea man Bernard Evans was 6 years old at the start of the war. As a child he lived in Baptist Well Street, Waun Wen, and went to the nearby St Joseph's Infant School. Here he recalls a young child's memories of the time he and his family were left homeless after a night of the German bombing raids. At the time, he, his mother and sister were sitting in the air-raid shelter in his back garden. That was when their house received a direct hit.

In the late 1940s, our family lived in Waun Wen. This was one of the Swansea areas that had always been considered as a prime target for the enemy bombers. This was because of its close proximity to the Cwmfelin Steel Works. On the night of the blitz, as soon as we heard the sound of the air-raid warning siren, we left the house. I made my way with my parents and my 8-year-old sister to the Anderson shelter we had erected in the back garden. Once we were inside, my father brought out a large steel hoarding board normally used for advertising Lyons tea. As he always did, he placed it at an angle across the entrance to the shelter, which faced the house. He then anchored the hoarding to the ground with some sandbags and piles of earth. It was only then we all believed we were safe.

We sat quietly in the darkness. Then, after what seemed to be just a short time, we heard the aircraft approaching overhead. The sounds were followed by loud bangs and crackling sounds as the incendiary bombs hit the earth and walls around the shelter. Suddenly, there came an almost deafening bang. I could feel the blast from the impact of the explosion as it shook the ground and the shelter beneath us.

I can remember clearly sitting there and hearing the pieces of metal clattering against the surface of the hoarding in front of our shelter. We were all terrified, obviously, but my mother managed to stay calm enough to tell us it was better for us to stay inside the shelter, even though by then everything had gone quiet. Eventually, we heard noises outside. I recognised the voice of my older brother. He had stayed the night with our aunt so we were all relieved to know that each one of us was all right. Slowly, we emerged from the shelter and stood together in total shock. I could see where once our house had stood now there was just a huge, empty space in between the row of terraced houses. We could also see that only the outer walls were left intact and that the fireplaces in the bedrooms were still visible. I could hear my father shouting beside me, 'Our house has gone.'

This was the time when homes had no fridges. My mother always kept the butter cool by placing the pack in a bowl of water stood on the kitchen floor. So, I suppose it was typical for my mother's first words on seeing the devastation were, 'And, to think I put a new half-pound of butter in that bowl last night.'

Even today, I walk through Baptist Well Street occasionally and see the two houses which replaced those bombed-out homes. My thoughts then go back to that night of the blitz.

Bernard with his sister Glenys, c. 1940. (Courtesy Bernard Evans)

After the destruction of our Waun Wen home, the Swansea Council rehoused the family in Mayhill. We were not there long before once again the incendiary bombs started falling on our garden. Like before, we had an Anderson shelter, but by now I think my parents had lost all faith in them.

By now, my father was in his early fifties and he had joined the Home Guard. I was always proud to see him in his uniform. As well as the Home Guard, he was also a fire-watcher. This entailed groups of men, some too young to fight and others too old. These men would patrol the streets of the locality during the air raids. Among their list of duties was looking out for fires started by incendiary bombs.

Then they had to take the steps necessary to put the fires out. Sometimes during an air raid, the group of men were forced to dive for cover to avoid the falling bombs. During one such explosion, one of the men, a lad of 17 years old, lost his arm when a burning building collapsed on him. I can recall an occasion when my father took me to see the gun site where he was based that was on Ashleigh Road, near Blackpill, although at the time I do not remember being impressed by it at all. I do not think that as a 7-year-old I was old enough to appreciate the purpose of all the guns and activity.

Back at our new home in Mayhill, the air raids continued and now it was only my mother to look after my sister and me. We no longer used the air-raid shelter in the garden. As soon as the first air-raid warning had sounded, my mother would get us children together. We would hurry from Mayhill down the steep Waun Wen road. Then we all stayed in the large communal air-raid shelter that was underneath St Joseph's Church, near my school in Llangyfelach Street. As a child, I did not appreciate the distance I had to walk with my mother and sister so regularly. Nor did I realise that my mother's parents lived directly opposite and so close to the shelter. It is only now as an adult that I can see the point of it all.

My mother must have felt safer being closer to her family and friends. At the time, I did not appreciate having to walk for over a mile to get to the air-raid shelter. Now I realise what lengths my mother and my father went through to keep our family safe.

After the war, Bernard went on to grammar school and then to work for the Swansea Council for over forty years.

CHAPTER SIXTEEN

The Probert Family

The Cwm, 1950s. Castle Craig on the summit was destroyed in a gale in recent times.
(Courtesy Haydn Probert)

Swansea man Haydn Probert now lives in Leicester. He tells his story of what it was like as a child growing up in Swansea during the war:

When the war started, I was a child living in Cwm Road in the Hafod. After our house was bombed, we moved to Robert Street. It is the time I recall the numerous times when, during the air raids, my older sister woke me up from bed. Then she took my hand and guided me to a neighbour, Mrs Scott's house, which was two doors away from ours. There I sat on my mother's lap as we all gathered in Mrs Scott's front room. In the early days of the war, I went with my brother to a lock-up garage in Elgin Street, Manselton. This is the place from where we collected our Mickey Mouse gas masks. The garage was also used as an ARP post. I also remember the Swansea Council workers taking all the railings from outside the houses to help make wartime ammunition. As the war went on, concrete air-raid shelters appeared in Manor Road and Cecil Street, although I do not recall seeing them anywhere else.

There was an ARP warden who stood guard every night on the corner of Robert Street. I used to see him from my bedroom window. Where he stood, there was a sign on the wall painted 'EWS' in large letters. The sign indicated there was an emergency water supply nearby for use by the fire brigade. The actual water tank was situated at the back of the houses in Robert Street that had been bombed. At one time, I went out to the garden to play and I could see a barrage balloon that always seemed to be hovering above our house.

The emergency ambulances also passed through the streets regularly. These were small vans which were coloured Air Force blue. The vehicles had no doors at the back and only a black curtain to cover the rear of the vehicle. Another time, I was standing in the middle of Robert Street and a plane flew right over our heads. As it was only just above the rooftops of the houses, I stood with my brother waving to the pilot that I could see clearly, as he was flying so low.

Although I have no clear memories of hearing the air-raid sirens or the sound of any bombing, I know that many people died during the bombing raids. The bombers demolished a whole row of terraced houses that stood opposite our house in Robert Street. That is except for one house that remained intact at each end of the terrace. The bombing also left a huge crater at the back of the street where the houses had stood. There was also a large crater with two air-raid shelters, which had been built inside it, in Manselton Park. We kids used to play on the high ground that had once been, and was still known locally as, 'the race course', which is just behind the steep slopes of the park. This is where many Americans were stationed during the war.

After the war, there was still a lot of barbed-wire fencing around the whole area. We lads were always cutting ourselves trying to climb through. Many of my friends bought American army gaiters from Millets store. The gaiters came up to the knees and saved them from injuries. Alas, I did not have gaiters. My mother kept telling me off for cutting my legs on the barbed-wire fences. After the war, we children played on the bombed building sites in Robert Street, where there was a crater. I was always finding money, old clothes or toys.

On VE Day, I stood behind Mr Haynes, one of our neighbours, while he painted a big 'V for Victory' sign. The white sign stretched from one side of Manor Road to the centre of Major Street. It was great on VE Day with all the street parties and lots of singing and dancing. Like many of the children, I had never seen a street party before. Naturally, we were too young to realise the significance and the historic event of the celebrations. We were far more overwhelmed by the sight of so much shouting, laughing and crying people gathered in one place.

Just after the end of the war, some Canadian Welfare people came to our Manselton Infants' School. They stood in the school hall handing out chocolate to the pupils. The chocolate was a powder that looked like cocoa, which we could turn into drinks, although I always ate my share with a spoon, straight from the container. The teachers instructed all the schoolchildren to bring back any tins or containers they could from home. The welfare people then filled them up with chocolate. My brother and I collected six large baby-food tins. The next day we took three each to school and watched them being filled up with chocolate. We children had not seen anything like sweets or chocolate for years. We were almost crazy with delight. For weeks after, we ate the chocolate and knew when the tins were empty the 'nice ladies' would fill them up again. Another kind of food we kids ate was dried egg that came from America. It was a yellow powder that came in boxes and eaten mixed with water. I loved the taste of it even better than real eggs. Then we had a powdered potato called 'Pom'. It looked like mashed potato when it was on the plate. Yet, to me, the white slushy mix was the worst thing ever tasted, even for a war baby.

Haydn's brother, Albert Probert, recalls:

I was living with my family at Cwm Road in the Hafod when the war began. I was 14 years old, which in those days was the normal school-leaving age. At the time, I had just started working as a shop assistant for Eddie James, at his butcher's shop, which was in the Pentre. The worse night I can remember of the war occurred on Friday night, 17 January 1941. It was the time when during the bombing raid a row of houses in the Hafod was hit and twenty families, including a family of eight, were killed. During the same raid, my own family was bombed out of our home. Our family was moved to a temporary house in Manor Road, where we stayed for about three weeks. That was before we were moved again to another address in Robert Street. Sadly, this time it also meant that the family had to be split up. Some of the children were taken to my aunt's house in Manor Road. Some of us went to live at my grandmother's house in Yschyborfach Street. Finally, we moved to

Robert Street. It is while we were living there, I joined the 12th Glamorgan Home Guard unit that was based in Treboeth, although it finished in 1944, when the Home Guard was stood down.

Even though times were hard, people still tried to believe there was some humour too. I can recall one funny incident while I was in the Home Guard. There was one night when I was making my way home from Treboeth. I had my Home Guard rifle over my shoulder and I was walking along Manor Road, Manselton. Suddenly, even in the blacked-out street, I could see there were three police officers standing in the middle of the road.

As I drew closer, one of them shouted over to ask if I had my rifle with me. When I replied 'yes' the officer asked me to come over to them. As soon as I did so, they started shouting in the direction of a house, 'Come on out, and don't resist, we have a man with a gun here.'

With that, I saw a man who came out of the house with his hands up above his head. Apparently, the man had been caught burgling it.

Throughout the war years, I saw quite a few planes flying over Swansea. I also have vivid memories of the devastation of the town centre. Naturally, we were relieved when the war ended and people celebrated. By then, I was working at the ICI. Then, as it happened for so many others, I had to leave the job. This was when all the men returned from the forces and reclaimed their pre-war occupations.

Violet Probert, Albert's wife, was living in Margaret Street in St Thomas at the outbreak of the war. She remembers:

My name then was Violet Hollet. I was 14 years old, the school-leaving age in those days. I was working as a shop assistant for Matthews, the florist's shop, that was in Oxford Street. Because the area where we lived was so close to the docks, it meant that the nearby Kilvey Hill and the surrounding area regularly suffered bomb damage from air raids. Although the prime targets of the bombers were the docks, the surrounding areas of St Thomas, Bonymaen and the Hafod suffered all the bombs that missed. The raids began with parachute flares falling silently on Kilvey Hill. A large number of incendiary bombs followed, and which fell on both sides of the River Tawe. The continuous bombing was kept up from the early evening until after midnight. One of the bombing raids wiped out a whole family in Port Tennant Road.

During the air raids, we families all fled to what we believed was the safety of the air-raid shelter, which was in our back garden. At one time, during such a raid, an incendiary came into our back kitchen. As going to work meant I walked from St Thomas to Oxford Street each day, I remember feeling sad at the destruction of the town. Wherever I looked, all I could see was rubble and burnt-out buildings that had once been a lovely town. I could see that whole streets, rows of shops and the market had disappeared. There were craters and firefighters' hoses and debris covering a huge area of the town centre, especially around Castle Street.

When it came to VE Day, I watched as our neighbours and friends began arranging the street parties. I can also remember seeing all the bunting going up. A friend and I went down to join the thousands of people who had gathered to dance on the green at the Guildhall. We were grateful to celebrate the end of the war.

Donald Probert, Haydn's brother, now living in Penlan, recalls:

I was living in Cwm Road, Hafod, and was 4 years old when the war broke out. But I do remember playing outside the house, then someone rushing me to the Cwmfelin air-raid shelter when the warning siren went off. I can also recall other times when I was pushed into the air-raid shelter that was under Libanus Chapel in Cwmbwrla Square. After we were bombed out, I moved with my family to Manor Road. From there we moved to Robert Street. I can remember going with my brothers to fetch our gas masks from the ARP post in Elgin Street. By the time the war ended, I was at Cwmbwrla Junior Boys School. Later, I went on to Manselton Senior School and left in 1950.

Sheila Probert, Donald's wife, remembers:

I was in Gorse Infants' School when the war began. I was not very old but I can recall going into the air-raid shelter, which was underneath the school. I also recall my mother pushing me to the shelter in the garden. I cried, not only because I did not like the shelter, it was because I preferred the shelter next door that had a piano in it. I suppose I wanted to join in the singing that we could hear sometimes coming from the shelter next door. But I cried again when I had to leave the shelter with the sound of the all-clear.

When the war began, Haydn's sister Barbara was living with her family at Cwm Road, Hafod. She recalls the night when her family was left homeless by the bombers:

On Friday 17 January 1941, I was sitting quietly with my family and never thought it would be the last time I would see my home. We were all inside the living room when the bombs started to fall all around us. Naturally, we were terrified. In minutes, we were all rushing from the living room into the garden. Each house had an air-raid shelter. All the shelters were set up in the garden. Now, unlike many back gardens that had walls or fences, the gardens in Cwm Road had been built with no dividing walls. When the bombing began, like us, everybody ran out of the neighbouring houses to the air-raid shelters that were in their gardens. As a 7-year-old child at the time, I panicked and ran, too. In

Haydn Probert and his late wife Jacqueline. (Courtesy Haydn Probert)

the confusion, I ran into the next garden by mistake and ended up in the wrong shelter. It was the same moment that the bombs hit our house and when other houses were bombed, too. People were screaming as some of the buildings fell onto the shelter that I was in, and then the roof of the shelter caved in. The doorway to the shelter was blocked by falling debris and rubble, and I was buried inside. The rescuers had to come and dig me out. It seemed like hours before I was free and my family finally knew I was safe.

Soon after that, my brother and I were evacuated to a farm in Llanarthne in Carmarthen. We went to school there and had to walk one and a half miles there and back. It was a long way for us children, who had been used to the five-minute walk to our old school. Sometimes after school we waited hopefully for the local mail van, which often stopped to pick us up. If the van did not turn up so we had to keep on walking. We were both there for about twelve months. When we came back to Swansea, I went to Cwmbwrla Junior School, then to the Manselton Senior Girls' School. The day the war ended, we all sang our thanks in the school assembly hall. I remember there was a huge street party in Robert Street where the family lived then and together we all celebrated VE Day.

Richard Squires, Barbara's husband, recalls:

I was 12 years old, a pupil in Manselton Boys' School when the war started. Every day after school I used to jump on my bike and go to my job as a paperboy, which meant cycling into the town centre and selling papers. On one particular day I was in Castle Street when an air raid began, and I rushed for the town's communal air-raid shelter. The nearest one was in College Street. It was in the crypt of the ill-fated Wesley Chapel. The basement of the chapel was situated on the corner of Swansea's old Goat Street, one of the many streets destroyed in the blitz. It was one of the many buildings that had been requisitioned as a public air-raid shelter at the start of the war. It was also a place where hundreds of people congregated socially. This is because of its well-known use as a fish and chips and as a refreshments bar. You had to go down about forty steps to the large shelter, which was at the bottom of the

Barbara and Richard Squires.

building. There were about fifty other people there by the time I came in. At the top of the stairs, there was a little cubicle selling snacks such as tea, pop, biscuits and crisps. It was popular and usually crowded, as you could imagine. So, after being in the shelter for a while, I decided to go upstairs and get some pop.

I had just turned from the cubicle and started to make my way down when a bomb dropped outside, just missing the church. However, the blast blew me off my feet and sent me flying down the flight of stairs. Even then, I considered myself lucky that I did not break my neck. On the following night, I thought of myself as being luckier still. Hundreds of people died when the Wesleyan Chapel took a direct hit, although there were many who survived. This was when officials had taken earlier measures to evacuate the building and lead people from the shelter to the safety of the stone arches that crossed the Strand.

As a paperboy I sold papers around Oxford Street and in the local public houses. I saw quite a lot of the American soldiers, and they used to give me chocolate and packets of chewing gum. As I was only 12 years old at the time, I was scared by the constant threats of air raids. There was the time when I heard that a bomb had dropped near Castle Street, but that it had not exploded. We all went down in the hope of seeing it, but we found the police had cordoned off the area. So we all stood [and watched] the action of the soldiers as they lifted the bomb. Then, just as they were carrying the bomb towards the lorry to take it away, it went off. All the soldiers were killed before our eyes. As I kept walking about the town selling papers, I noticed how I was seeing fewer of the town's fine buildings left standing by the day. Bit by bit, the town of my childhood had disappeared and I knew nothing would ever be the same.

Emrys Probert, Haydn's brother, was 10 years old when the war started. He lived with his family in the Cwm and was a pupil at Waun Wen School. After his family home was bombed he lived in Manor Road. While he was there, he saw American soldiers up at the racecourse, which is behind Manselton Park. Emrys recalls:

No one ever got to know the Americans or ever talked to them as there were different groups of them who came and went almost every day. When I was

Manor Road where the Probert family stayed after being bombed out of their home in the Cwm. The large building, centre, was Manselton Secondary Modern School.

11 years old, I was evacuated with my sister to a farm in Llanarthne in Carmarthen. Once, when we were on the farm, a friend and I went into where the farmer kept chickens. There was no sound in the barn, so my friend climbed up the side of the building. As he reached the loft, a chicken pecked him hard on the forehead. We came back to Swansea in 1942. By then, the worst of the air raids were over and I started work in the Cwmfelin Steel Works. I remember going into town. I could not believe the damage that had been done to such a lovely town.

Nancy, Emrys's wife, remembers:

I was living in Clydach when the war began. I was in the Globe Cinema when the air-raid siren went off. We all had to run to the air-raid shelter, which was at the side of the Clydach Fire Station. My uncle was in the army so I rode my bike down to the Mond to wave him off to the war. I had to walk from Sunnybank to Clydach to go to school. The adults always came with us in case there was an air raid. Sometimes we took the bus to Swansea, but I felt terrible seeing the devastation of the town. There was an American camp at Craig Cefn Park, and we found the Americans were always very polite. I was in Clydach on VE Day. We were all happy and all the children went to the Globe Cinema. There we children were each given a banana, the first banana I had ever seen.

Albert and Violet Probert.
(Courtesy Haydn Probert)

Donald and Sheila Probert.
(Courtesy Haydn Probert)

Emrys and Nancy Probert.
(Courtesy Haydn Probert)

CHAPTER SEVENTEEN
Peggy Morgan

Peggy Morgan's father-in-law, Dan, owned the renowned bicycle store in Oxford Street. The shop was bombed twice during the war. (Courtesy South Wales Evening Post*)*

Peggy Morgan lives in Mumbles, the picturesque village where she has lived for most of her life. In the mid-1970s, she and her husband Herbert Morgan were elected as the first Conservative mayors of Swansea. During their mayoral term of office, Peggy and her husband faced many challenging occasions. As Peggy recalls, there were the good times, too. She and her husband attended many hospital and civic functions, and were responsible for many changes, including the welcome free bus travel for Swansea pensioners.

Herbert Morgan was the son of Dan Morgan, the owner of the renowned bicycle business. As with many of the local firms that had been established in the town for decades, the Dan Morgan bike shop was considered to be an institution. The shop had stood for decades on the site opposite the old and long-demolished National School in Oxford Street. The shop was bombed twice during the blitz, after which Mr Morgan did not have the heart to open up for business again. Recalling her own memories of the Second World War, Peggy remembers the time when she

Peggy Morgan, Mayoress of Swansea, 1975–6. (Courtesy Peggy Morgan)

walked around the town and saw the damaged buildings after the blitz. There was one point when she stood amazed by the sight of a huge crater in the middle of Dillwyn Street.

As a young woman, Peggy lived with her family in Langland Road, a few miles from the picturesque Langland Bay. Every day throughout the war years, Peggy made the journey to work by the Mumbles Train, changing about halfway to what was then a long and tedious bus ride to her workplace. This was at the Mond Nickel Works at Clydach, a refinery company responsible for much of the employment and housing built in Clydach. Peggy worked as an assistant in the accounts department, which like many businesses had been evacuated from London. Peggy recounts one wartime experience:

As we worked in the office, our tasks were interrupted constantly by the sound of the air-raid warning sirens. It meant that we all had to make our way to the

Herbert Morgan, Mayor of Swansea, 1975–6. (Courtesy Peggy Morgan)

air-raid shelters. However, we young girls walked around, or else we stood watching the aeroplanes as they flew low towards the Swansea Docks. One day, during such a break, we noticed an aeroplane which we recognised had French markings on the side of it. We could see the markings clearly, because the plane was flying so low. We girls even stood and waved to the pilot. Then, later on, we heard that a plane had gone down to the docks and, without warning, it had machine-gunned a large number of dock workers who had been working on the quayside.

Peggy's wartime account of this incident describes what was later recorded as one of Swansea's first air raids, on Wednesday 10 July 1940, the day when a single enemy plane approached Swansea Docks. The well-documented incident describes how the bomber dropped four high-explosive bombs at the 'Mole' end of the King's Dock. The surprising nature of the daylight attack also meant there were many workers on duty. As there was no alert to the imminent air strike, many people were killed. At the same time, the dock sheds and workshops were damaged.

Peggy also recalls another time at home:

During the blitz, I was sitting with friends in the Tivoli Cinema in Mumbles, watching the film. Suddenly, a public warning came up on the screen. This was a message which appeared on the cinema screens regularly during the war. The message advised patrons that they could leave the cinema, or stay if they wanted. I left, thinking I would be safer to try and get back to my home as soon as possible, although it was only once I was outside that I realised how serious things were. When I reached Oystermouth Square, we could see there were incendiary bombs falling down all over the area. We all rushed home to Langland Road.

Peggy's work in the accounts department was considered a reserved occupation. Yet she was still among the many hundreds of people to volunteer for war work. Peggy joined the Auxiliary Fire Service unit that was based in Mumbles. There, she was one of three office workers who took turns to help. In Oystermouth, during wartime, the local residents soon came to recognise that if the church bells rang it was a sign that an air raid was imminent. They also learned by the sound that the enemy planes flew from their German bases to Liverpool and the north-west coastline. They went there and back every Friday night. It meant that any bombs that were left over after the night-time bombing raids were dropped haphazardly across the width of Swansea Bay.

CHAPTER EIGHTEEN

Joan Bevan

Rhossili Bay, where Joan met her future husband, Ken Bevan, in 1940. They were married at St Mary's Church, centre, on 14 December 1946.

Joan Bevan lives in Killay, which has been her home since 1937. She enjoys being with her sons and her grandchildren, who live nearby. She loves taking walks along the Mumbles coastline and making trips to the local Gower bays. Joan's most striking wartime memories begin one day in 1940. That was the day when her new boyfriend Ken, who lived in the Gower village of Rhossili, gave her the bad news that he had been called up to join the RAF. She was devastated for a while, until she told herself, 'Well, I am going to join up and be with him.'

Without hesitation, Joan made the trip to the YMCA, where she signed up to join the WAAF. 'Not one of my wisest of decisions,' Joan recalls, because she soon discovered that Ken had been dispatched to India. However, it was wartime and life went on. Joan worked as a teleprinter operator, which involved her in the tasks of sending signals underground from the Kodak building in London. As time went by, Joan was promoted to the rank of corporal. There was one memorable occasion when she 'sent a signal which brought Sir Winston Churchill back to England from Africa'.

Then one day an officer informed Joan that she was being transferred to Scotland. Her first reaction was to tell the officer, 'No, I am not going there.'

Joan joined the WAAF in 1940. (Courtesy Joan Bevan)

He gave her leave of absence so she could come home to Swansea and think it over. Finally, with great reluctance, she made the journey north. Joan still remembers the day she left when her father drove her to High Street station. Her mother insisted that she packed some hard-boiled eggs and a pillow in her kitbag.

At the time of the Swansea Blitz, Joan was a young girl working for a firm of solicitors, Gee and Edwards, which had premises in St Mary's Square. She recalls that on the third night of the blitz she had been one of the last of the staff to leave her office and make her way home. As she crossed the square to post some letters, she looked around the busy street and never realised that this would be the last time she would see the town or her workplace as she had always known it. After posting the letters, she made her way towards the bus station in Singleton Street. Joan recalls that when she arrived at the bus station she could see that every bus stop was packed with hundreds of people. Many of them were doing their best to get out of town rather than face another night of the bombing raids in an area that was so much at risk. Joan decided to telephone her father from a call box and asked him to come and pick her up. He drove her home in his car, where they had tea of a boiled egg and some bread and butter. Then together they left the house and drove off to a friend's house in Llanelli, where she and her father stayed for the rest of the night.

The following day, Joan's father drove her back to Swansea in good time for her to start her day's work. Joan arrived in St Mary's Square and was shocked to find the whole area was one great morass of destruction. Wherever she looked, there were firefighting hoses and mounds of smouldering rubble. Burnt-out shells stood in place of what had once been fine buildings. She recalls:

I felt so sad to see the familiar shops and streets of my childhood destroyed beyond all recognition. Even worse was knowing that my office where I had worked and made so many friends had gone. The blitz had not only destroyed my workplace, but, as it had for many people, my future livelihood had been destroyed, too.

Joan's father was an auxiliary coastguard stationed at Rhossili during the years of the war. It was while she was visiting him that she and her friends decided they would take a walk along the almost vertical Gower cliff top. Joan recounts how they were about halfway along the track when they heard voices calling and realised that some of the young men of Rhossili had noticed them: 'I remember the one who came and sat next to me had auburn hair and wore brightly coloured trousers to match. He said, "Come for a walk." That is how I first met Kenny, from the nearby Rhossili Tea Rooms, who became my husband.'

Joan and Ken were married on a sunny 14 December 1946. She describes how she had stood proudly in her wedding dress as she entered the beautiful St Mary's Church at Rhossili. 'Sadly, Ken died twenty-three years ago. Today, I am so grateful to have my family around me,' she says.

Joan Bevan beside Swansea Bay with Mumbles in the background, 2006. (Courtesy Joan Bevan)

CHAPTER NINETEEN

Mabel Irene Ogilvie

Medical staff inspect the damage to Swansea General Hospital after the final bombing raid on the city, 16 February 1943. (Courtesy South Wales Evening Post)

Mabel Irene Ogilvie (née Thomas) was born in the Lake District and served in the Land Army in West Wales during the war. Her husband Stanley was born in Gowerton and served in the Royal Marine Corps. On obtaining a civil-service post in Swansea they both moved to Killay, where they have lived since the 1960s. This is an account of Mabel's wartime experiences in the Land Army, in which she is happy to 'relive the experiences all over again with the happy memories of parts of it'.

Mabel was 20 years old when war was declared. Her father, a Royal Navy reservist, was called up immediately as a chief petty officer. Mabel remembers spending the early days of the war sitting in the Anderson shelter listening to the enemy planes flying overhead and wondering where the next bomb was going to land. Then in 1941, when young women were being drafted into war work, Mabel decided to join the Women's Land Army (WLA). It seemed to offer a healthy outdoor life as well as enabling the menfolk working on the land to be called up for military duties. On joining, Mabel found herself posted with thirty other land girls to a WLA hostel in Pembrokeshire, where the housekeeper was in charge of them. They were taken out daily by lorry to work on the land, with a packed lunch of beetroot or cheese sandwiches.

Mabel hated these sandwiches almost as much as her duties of potato picking, hedge trimming and corn threshing, which she found to be 'very dirty and uncomfortable work'. Undeterred, Mabel applied successfully for a move to Pentre Mansion in a neighbouring village. There she worked in the greenhouses, thinning grapes, picking the soft fruits and preparing the surplus for sale. At this time, the mansion was owned by the Saunders-Davis family. It was commandeered by the military authorities for use as an auxiliary hospital and convalescence home for sick and wounded servicemen. It was to Pentre that Royal Marine Stanley Ogilvie came as a patient to recover from his war injuries, and into Mabel's life. They were married in 1947. Three years later, their identical twins Dilys and Glenys were born.

OPERATION WASSERVOGEL

This is a brief extract from an account of 'Operation Wasservogel' (Waterbird), which Mabel Ogilvie recalls was passed on to her husband many years ago. It is the story of the final German air raid on Swansea, on 16 February 1943.

For most people, Tuesday 16 February 1943 was just another day in the war. At Eindhoven, aircraft of KG2 prepared for a raid on Swansea. While these preparations were being made, across the Channel to bomb Swansea, another group drawn from all parts of Britain and the Commonwealth was preparing to meet them. The Royal Air Force station at Fairwood Common had opened in June 1941 and came under No.10 Group Fighter Command. Its area of operations included parts of the Bristol Channel, the Irish Sea and the south-west corner of Wales, and some of the most beautiful coastal scenery in Britain.

Hundreds of lorry-loads of hard core formed the foundations of the three runways. The aircraft included Defiants, Turbinlite Havocs and Beaufighters. The buildings belonging to the station were located in Upper Killay and to the south of Fairwood Lodge.

The Operations Room was originally in Weig Fach Lane, between Cockett and Fforestfach. In the spring of 1943 it was moved to a new location in Hen Parc. The motto of the squadron was 'Numquam domandi' (Never be tamed), a suitable motto for a group of flyers who put fear into the hearts of the Luftwaffe aircrew. A few of the pilots were accommodated in the large Gower country houses, Parc le Breos and Kilvrough Manor, both within walking distance of one of the most picturesque Gower settings of Three Cliffs Bay.

The targets on the night were Swansea Docks – in particular, the Queen's Dock, King's Dock and the Prince of Wales Dock. Queen's Dock was used mainly by tankers and had oil-storage tanks adjacent to it. The other two docks were coal and coke and general cargo surrounded by the GWR marshalling yards. The weather forecast was good and the sky was clear with a full moon. The first warning of the air raid was received at Fairwood Common at 21.47 hours. Following stiff opposition from the anti-aircraft guns and the night-fighters, several aircraft turned back. After seven months without a raid, this raid came as a shock to everyone, although the main target of the docks remained untouched. The damage followed the line from the Hafod and St Thomas areas, Brynymor Road and across the seafront. The bombs falling in the St Helen's Road area caused serious damage to the General Hospital. One of the wards was demolished completely, and an operating theatre was put out of use. Over 300 patients were evacuated to other hospitals. A bomb-disposal officer was killed when a bomb which fell at the entrance to the casualty ward exploded the next day.

The deaths of three young women in the Women's Auxiliary Air Force at Fairwood Common was recorded as especially poignant. This is because all three had only recently enlisted, even though the pay of an Aircraft Woman Second Class was one shilling and ten pence a day. Thus, in just three hours during the night of Swansea's last air raid, thirty-five civilians, three WAAFs and several German airmen all died as a result of the KG2 abortive attempt to bomb Swansea Docks.

Mabel Irene Ogilvie, 2004.
(Courtesy Mabel Ogilvie)

CHAPTER TWENTY

Gorseinon Men at War

John Beck Owen was the 108th truck driver to enter Berlin. He is photographed with his regiment when they were building bridges across a river in Germany. (Courtesy Gorseinon Archive and History Society)

William Gear was captured in Tobruk and was involved in the long march from North Africa to Italy, where thousands of prisoners of war died en route of starvation. After the fall of Italy he was transferred back to Britain. (Courtesy Gorseinon Archive and History Society)

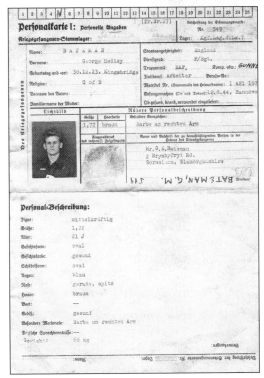

Hedley Bateman was a warrant officer in the RAF, and served in Bomber Command. He was a gunner, flying in the Lancaster Bombers, when his plane was shot down over Hanover. He baled out, but was taken prisoner by the Germans and celebrated his 21st birthday as a prisoner of war. Later, he was taken by rail through Berlin and travelled further east. Hedley escaped a number of times, but was always recaptured and transferred to various German camps before he finally returned to Britain. Left: Hedley Bateman's prisoner-of-war documents. (Both images courtesy Gorseinon Archive and History Society)

CHAPTER TWENTY-ONE

Wyn Calvin and Wartime Entertainment

Wyn Calvin was a star performer at the Swansea Empire until its closure in 1957. He is renowned as the 'Welsh Prince of Laughter' and for his role as Britain's premier pantomime dame.
(Courtesy Wyn Calvin)

Wyn Calvin MBE and officer of the Order of St John, actor, comedian and broadcaster, is known as 'The Welsh Prince of Laughter' as well as 'Britain's premier pantomime dame'. For decades, his stage performances drew record crowds to the theatres. He was a well-loved and greatly admired star performer at the Swansea Empire Theatre before its closure in 1957. Here Wyn recalls ENSA, the wartime entertainment service, and his first professional engagement in 1945:

As soon as war was declared, the theatre and film producer Basil Dean was commissioned to mobilise entertainers of all types to provide 'morale-raising shows'. These shows were not only for men and women, in uniform, but also to appear in ammunition factory canteens, shipyards hospitals and later, during the blitz, the communal air-raid shelters. While London theatres closed for a while, the Theatre Royal in Drury Lane was available and became, for six years, the headquarters of the Entertainment National Service Association or ENSA – what the artistes called 'Every Night Something Atrocious'. This was not meant to be an assessment of the actual ENSA productions (though a motley crowd of singers, comedians, jugglers, dancers and seaside concert-party artistes were often thrown together into a variety of shows). It gave more than 2½ million performances during its existence. The conditions under which artistes were expected to perform varied between shipyards or factories, or else, tiny halls, or even the backs of a lorry.

Britain was blacked out and there was no street lighting after dark. All signposts, town names and railway-station identities had been removed. Therefore, finding the locations for the next wartime performances was perplexing to say the least. Abroad, during the 'phoney war', when the BEF [the British Expeditionary Force], was in France, some of the biggest names of the day volunteered to lead the ENSA parties. They included highly paid performers like Will Hay, George Formby, Tommy Trinder, Will Fyffe and Evelyn Laye. They accepted the salary of just £10 a week (the ENSA maximum) to entertain those serving in the war in France and Belgium. Gracie Fields was actually singing 'We're Going to Hang Out the Washing on the Siegfried Line' a few miles away from that 'impregnable defence'.

The renowned Welsh comedienne Gladys Morgan (who appeared in the family act with her husband and daughter Joan) remembered the smallest audience – it was on a lighthouse.

Gladys's high-pitched laugh, which tickled Swansea listeners in the days of the top-rating radio programme *Welsh Rarebit* re-echoed as she recalled the setting. 'This lighthouse was just off the

ENSA poster for the 1945 revue for British Forces in France, Belgium, Holland and Germany.
(Courtesy Wyn Calvin)

Northumbrian coast and we played to two people – the lighthouse keeper and his daughter.' Joan added to the story with 'She didn't look a bit like Grace Darling.'

Calvin continues his account:

As the areas of wartime conflict increased around the world so the ENSA shows followed the forces to North Africa, Egypt, Persia, Malta, Cyprus, India and Malaya, Singapore, Italy and then France again. Sometimes it was a play with a West End cast; a Shakespeare production headed by Donald Wolfit. At other times, it would be just a duo visiting hospitals. Joyce Grenfell with her pianist was one splendid example. However, mostly it would be a variety show with dancing girls, a comedian, a speciality act and a musician or two.

Calvin's own ENSA experience came in early 1945:

As a teenager, straight from school, I was already 'theatre crazy'. I was booked as the 'juvenile' in a revue show with ten girls and a comedian. This meant that we were to play at leave centres in France, Belgium and the newly liberated Holland. Because of the possibility of capture by the enemy, the ENSA artists overseas had to wear a uniform. However, the very day that I, as a callow youth, was put into the military-style uniform, Hitler committed suicide.

Calvin goes on how to describe how he was soon playing in Germany:

At an ENSA hostel one evening, a company of well-known actors from the Old Vic arrived, led by Sir Laurence Olivier. They had all just experienced a stormy sea crossing, and were to rest for a few hours before travelling over the bomb-

and battle-shattered roads further into Germany. The younger members of the company were very attentive to the older actor, who had obviously had a bad crossing too. Seeing their concern, I suggested they could use my room so that the member could rest more peacefully for a few hours. They graciously accepted and ever since I have been able to boast that Dame Sybil Thorndike slept in my bed.

ENSA ended in November 1945, when it was replaced by the CSE (Combined Services Entertainment).

An 18-year-old Wyn Calvin plays an elderly councillor in the revue By Your Leave, *1945. (Courtesy Wyn Calvin)*

CHAPTER TWENTY-TWO

Americans in Swansea

Operation Bolero was the code name that was given to the build-up of American troops and materials in Britain that began in 1942 in preparation for the Normandy invasion. This operation was to be the essential prerequisite to Operation Overlord, the anticipated liberation of Europe. As early as 1941, there were plans for US troops to occupy Iceland and to establish forward bases in Northern Ireland early in any future conflict with Germany. New military camps were established around towns in South Wales. Millions of tons of materials and hundreds of thousands of men were transported across the Northern Atlantic. By January 1944, over 750,000 US Army personnel had arrived in Britain.

The American troops and personnel were based at camps all over South Wales. Farmers' fields were requisitioned for massive dumps of guns, tanks, aircraft and ammunition as the build-up commenced. This force was to enter France as soon as possible after D-Day. On D-Day plus one (7 June 1944) elements of the 2nd Infantry Division were to embark from Swansea for landings on Omaha Beach. The Port of Swansea had a number of functions in Operation Bolero. It brought in men and materials from the United States. The areas around the port were used as the base for units of the 2nd Infantry Division. The result was that a substantial number of men and machines arrived in Swansea Docks for distribution to the numerous supply bases.

The arrival of the American soldiers in Swansea in mid-1942 meant a whole new infrastructure. Nigel Robins's writings (www.swanseahistoryweb.org.uk) explain how the American vehicles, particularly the tanks, were much larger than those of their British counterparts. It meant that new methods were sought to transport them on the country's railways. In addition, a massive range of supply and sustain systems was needed to support the American combat units. There was also a need to the support the American personnel who were used to manage the specialised port traffic that started to arrive in Swansea Docks.

American soldiers and jeeps in Swansea streets became a regular sight. Locals talk of the Americans being friendly and generous, throwing sweets and fruit to the local children. The majority of American soldiers who arrived in Britain worked side by side with the local population. Locals described them as hardworking and polite. During the week they visited the local cafés and bars, and weekends on the dance halls. They also regularly joined in the dancing at the Patti Pavilion in Victoria Park. The Americans had good memories of Swansea too.

American troops, c. 1944. (Courtesy Nigel Robins's Swansea History website)

Americans working on logs in Swansea Docks, c. 1944. (Courtesy Nigel Robins's Swansea History website)

William Saxelby was with the 3121st Signal Port Service Company US Army Signal Corps. He arrived in Swansea in May 1944 and, with his buddy Ralph Outten, he was billeted with Cyril Richards and his family in Cockett. William wrote:

I have great memories of the sing-songs in the parlour of the home we lived in, also in the side room of the local pub. I believe it was called the Lamb and Flag. We actually felt as part of the community and tried to supplement the wartime rations of the Richards with some items we could get from our quartermasters.

We were able to secure a Christmas turkey from a local butcher. It was a wonderful treat for men who had not been home for over a year. I will never forget 'leeks and the Sunday joint', which was usually lamb or occasionally beef.

William also explained how he and his wife have since attempted to trace Cyril Richards and his family. He also wrote: 'I am of English descent. There is a town in the Midlands by the same name as mine. I visited Saxelby while in the UK, although I enjoyed my visit to Wales even more.' *(Nigel Robins, www.swanseahistoryweb.org.uk)*

CHAPTER TWENTY-THREE

The Mametz Memorial and Battlefields Visits

In 1977, a group of local wartime researchers visited the Mametz Wood Red Dragon memorial in the Somme, where they laid a wreath in remembrance of the 700 members of the Swansea Battalion involved in an attack on Mametz Wood, 1916. These researchers – Tony Cook, John Powell, Peter Dover-Wade and Andrew Vollans – went on to form the Oystermouth History Travel Group in 1994 with the aim of researching the history of the large number of casualties from the Swansea area in both world wars.

Mametz Memorial. From left to right: Tony Cook, John Powell, Peter Dover-Wade, Andrew Vollans, 1977. (Courtesy Oystermouth History Travel Group)

Dover-Wade is the group's secretary, Powell is navigator and Cook is known as the 'diplomat'. Vollans, who has researched every name on the Swansea Cenotaph, is the group's 'knowledge base' and guide.

Their projects attracted so much local interest that the men decided to arrange formal tours of the battlefields in addition to their informal field trips to places well off the beaten track. Organised visits have included tours to Arnhem, Dunkirk, Normandy, Mons, Ypres and the Somme. Trips to Gallipoli, the Western Front and D-Day beaches are planned for the future, incorporating visits to the graves of local men. The group aims to further people's understanding of the tragedy of both world wars. It also does what it can to help the relatives and descendants of those involved to ensure their loved ones are always remembered, both at home and abroad.

Peter Dover-Wade will never forget his childhood friend Terry Absolom, one of the 387 people killed during the Swansea bombing raids of the Second World War. He recalls the second night of the Three Nights' Blitz, 20 February 1941: 'Terry came to call for me to play. My mother told him, "He won't be out tonight son, as they [the bombers] will be over soon."' Later that night a series of bombs hit the houses that stood near Peter's home on Mount Pleasant Hill. It was the last time he saw his young schoolfriend alive.

Bibliography

Alban, J.R. *Markets in Swansea*, Swansea, Swansea City Council, 1991
—— The *'Three Nights' Blitz*, City of Swansea, 1994
Gabb, G. *The Life and Times of the Swansea and Mumbles Railway*, Swansea, D. Brown and Sons Ltd, December 1994
Thomas, N.L. *The Story of Swansea's Markets: A history of their early beginnings down to the present day*, Swansea, N.L. Thomas, 1965

WEBSITE

Robins, N.A. www.swanseahistoryweb.org.uk, accessed 2004–6